The
RANCHO DE CHIMAYÓ
Cookbook

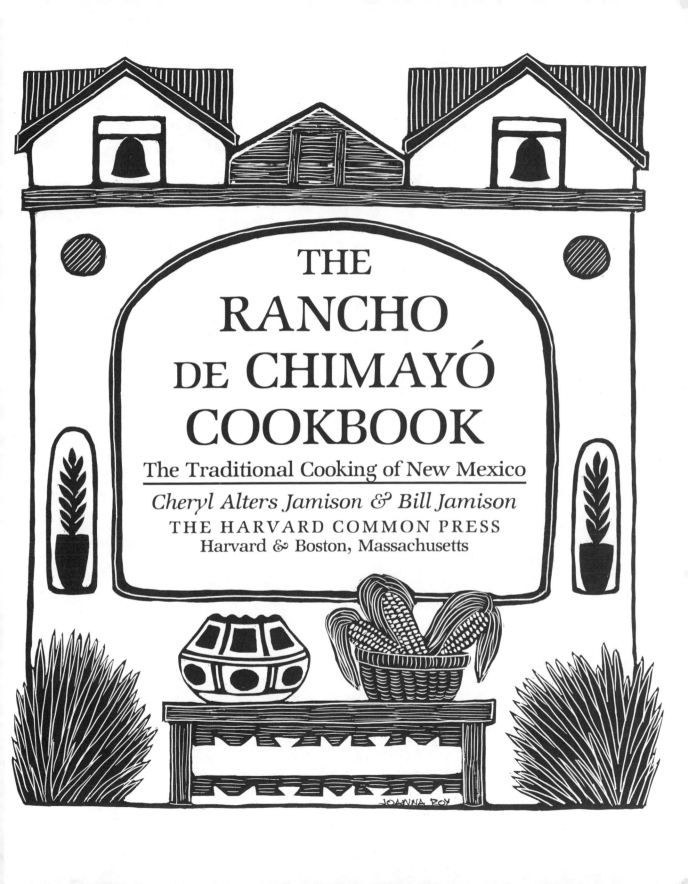

THE
RANCHO
DE CHIMAYÓ
COOKBOOK

The Traditional Cooking of New Mexico

Cheryl Alters Jamison & Bill Jamison

THE HARVARD COMMON PRESS
Harvard & Boston, Massachusetts

JOANNA ROY

The Harvard Common Press
535 Albany Street
Boston, Massachusetts 02118

Printed in the United States of America

LIBRARY OF CONGRESS CATALOGING-IN-PUBLICATION DATA

Jamison, Cheryl Alters.
    The Rancho de Chimayó cookbook : the traditional cooking of
New Mexico / Cheryl Alters Jamison & Bill Jamison.
        p.   cm.
    Includes index.
        ISBN 1-55832-040-7 : $18.95. — ISBN 1-55832-035-0 (pbk.) : $10.95
        1. Cookery—New Mexico. 2. Cookery, American—South-
western Style. 3. Rancho de Chimayó (Restaurant : Santa Fe,
N.M.) I. Jamison, Bill. II. Rancho de Chimayó (Restaurant :
Santa Fe, N.M.)
    III. Title.
    TX715.J3   1991
    641.59789—dc20   91-24777

Cover illustration by Mary Vander Molen
Cover design by Joyce C. Weston
Interior illustrations by Joanna Roy
Text design by Linda Ziedrich

10   9   8   7   6   5   4   3   2

For
LAUREN ALICIA JARAMILLO
*May you ennoble your heritage as profoundly
as your mother and grandparents have.*

The authors, CHERYL ALTERS JAMISON and BILL JAMISON, are New Mexico residents. They have been writing for over a decade on the history, arts, and food of the Southwest. They are experienced travel writers as well, co-authors of *Best Places to Stay in the Caribbean*, *Best Places to Stay in Hawaii*, and *Best Places to Stay in Mexico*, and the bestselling *Insider's Guide to Santa Fe* (Harvard Common Press).

The illustrator, JOANNA ROY, lives in New York. She studied at California State University, Long Beach, and at Barnard College, Parsons, The School of Visual Arts, and The Art Students League in New York. Her scratchboard illustrations appear in the *New York Times* and other newspapers, in *Travel & Leisure* and other magazines, and in books and calendars.

CONTENTS

ACKNOWLEDGMENTS

Many of the people who provided assistance to us are credited in the text, but some with important roles should be mentioned again, along with other key individuals. Barbara and Bill Richardson were the catalysts behind the entire project, though Eric Kampmann planted an early seed years ago. Julie and John Brueggeman provided one of the test kitchens and Betty and M. M. Alters aided us in testing recipes. Publisher Bruce Shaw and editor Dan Rosenberg contributed valuable advice and, with the rest of the Harvard Common Press staff, ardent support.

Arturo Jaramillo and Dan Jaramillo gave us immeasurable assistance with background and historical information. David Ortega, Ellen Bradbury, Susan Curtis, Peter Raub, Dr. Paul Bosland, Pat Trujillo Ovieda, Robert Martinez, and Jose C. de Baca also provided or confirmed material. Paula Lambert, Rob Coffland, and David Krutz contributed product information.

We appreciate the help of the entire restaurant staff, and must especially thank Josie Ortiz, Genoveva Martinez, Joan Medina, and Dave Bingham for their enthusiastic assistance with the recipes. Most of all, we acknowledge Florence and Laura Ann Jaramillo, the two people whose support and encouragement was absolutely essential to the project. Without them there wouldn't be a cookbook, and more importantly, not a Rancho de Chimayó.

RANCHO DE CHIMAYÓ
The Restaurant & Its Traditions

JOANNA ROY

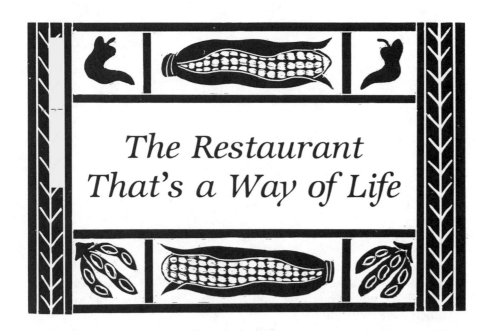

The Restaurant That's a Way of Life

Nobody forgets Rancho de Chimayó. The memories are often a collage of images. The homey adobe hacienda, radiantly warm and earthy. *Ristras* of red chile hanging from the roof around the front door. The glow on the terrace in the summer from the brilliant Southwestern sunset, or inside in the winter from one of the cozy corner fireplaces. Gracious hospitality, so guileless and genteel at the same time. Above all, the robust cooking, full of old-fashioned New Mexico country flavor—never bland, never dainty, never nouvelle.

Craig Claiborne remembered the hearty *carne adovada*, redolent of those fiery red chiles above the door. Maybe for you it's the *flautas*, the enchiladas, the tamales, the *posole*, or the densely luscious flan, one of the world's best versions of crème caramel. Almost everyone treasures the tastes of the fluffy *sopaipillas*, the unusual New Mexican bread served with most dishes.

As compelling as the food is, though, it's not quite the essence of the spell at Restaurante Rancho de Chimayó. The reason the restaurant is so memorable is that it is more than a restaurant. Arturo and Florence Jaramillo, the founders, envisioned it as a living tribute to the Spanish American heritage of New Mexico. In addition to the native cooking of the area, Rancho de Chimayó serves its guests a way of life.

When asked about the Jaramillos' goals a month before the 1965 opening, Arturo said, "I want this to be a different restaurant. I want the guests to feel they have been invited into an old Spanish home where the food and the atmosphere are in the grand early tradition." That was the inspiration years ago and it's still the effect. As Florence Jaramillo put it recently, "For all of us—not just the Jaramillo family, for all of us who appreciate this land and culture—this restaurant is one place the way of life here stays alive."

A new generation of family leadership shares the original vision. Laura Ann Jaramillo, Arturo and Florence's daughter, and her cousin, Dan Jaramillo, run the Restaurante today with Florence. Laura grew up immersed in the mission, helping her parents almost every day from the time she was seven—busing tables, serving food, washing dishes, even supervising some aspects of the operation as a teenager. Dan, who now assists Florence and Laura with management, started at the restaurant when he was in high school. A professional historian as well as a distinguished host, he is an expert on Chimayó's Spanish American legacy and is deeply devoted to its preservation.

Rancho de Chimayó cuts across the grain of our electronic age. While every corner of our global village rushes toward a future of uniformity and familiarity, the Jaramillos take us into a proud past, into a distinctive heritage little known outside New Mexico. Every aspect of the experience—the food, the mood, the setting, and the people—contributes harmoniously to a sense of timeless enchantment.

Today we often use the word "surprise" to describe something unpleasant and regularly apply "unique" to the ordinary. Not at Rancho de Chimayó. It remains a genuinely exceptional place and it retains the power to delight. That's why we never forget.

THE VISION

Arturo Jaramillo grew up in Chimayó in his grandparents' home, now converted to the Restaurante. When he was a child in the 1930s and '40s, the town was solidly rooted in its Spanish colonial past. The way of life was similar to what it had been for two centuries, not yet heavily influenced by automobiles, radios, and other twentieth-century changes.

Economic self-sufficiency had begun to give way to a cash economy, but every family continued to farm their land and raise most of their own food. Arturo's grandfather, Hermenegildo Martinez y Jaramillo, grew acres of chile, lots of corn and wheat, and some melons, carrots, and tomatoes. He maintained a fruit orchard, producing apples primarily, and a number of sheep, milk cows, pigs, and chickens. After the fall harvest he worked as a carpenter, specializing in pitched roofs. The family of eight had four weaving looms and kept them busy during the cold winters making wool cloth and blankets.

Despite the hardships of his Depression-era youth, Arturo loved the Chimayó of this period. He recalls the community as "rural, open, and neighborly," bound closely together by family ties, a strong common religion, economic interdependence, and a long, treasured heritage of Spanish colonial traditions.

It was the spirit and values of this time and place that Arturo and Florence set out to preserve at Rancho de Chimayó. The couple met after Arturo left New Mexico to serve in the Navy during the Korean War. French Canadian by ancestry, Florence was living in Connecticut, where the newlyweds settled originally. They visited Chimayó regularly and she soon came to share Arturo's attachment to the town and its culture.

Over the years the Jaramillos became increasingly disturbed by the changes they saw happening in the historic community. Financial and social pressures of many kinds were undermining the old ways. Living in the East, they were familiar with colonial preservation efforts in places such as Williamsburg, Virginia, and Sturbridge, Massachusetts. By the early 1960s they decided Chimayó would benefit from a similar project and they moved to New Mexico with Laura—just a toddler at the time—to initiate it.

Arturo's childhood home seemed the perfect spot. When his grandfather died in 1959 the Jaramillos had inherited a sixth of the 18-acre *rancho*. The other heirs didn't want the property for themselves and were happy to sell their interests to Arturo and Florence on generous terms.

The Jaramillos had a visionary plan for the house and land, as ambitious as any undertaking in Chimayó since the construction of the town's fortified plaza in the eighteenth century. They intended to use the old plaza as a model for a reconstructed colonial village, a living museum that would display authentic artifacts of the New Mexico heritage. The blueprints included a chapel, grist mills, farming implements, a 12-room lodge in the style of Spanish frontier homes, and a dining room serving the New Mexican dishes of Arturo's youth.

The concept was too bold for bankers, though one institution finally agreed to finance the refurbishing of the ancestral house for the restaurant portion of the plan. Arturo and Florence accepted the offer as a good beginning on their project and later found they could accomplish their goals through the restaurant and a kindred inn. At the same time, they discovered another important fact: opening and operating the kind of restaurant they wanted was a monumental mission in itself.

THE TWIN HACIENDAS

In retrospect, the decision to convert the grandparents' home to a restaurant was clearly a stroke of genius. In the early stages, though, the implementation of the idea seemed more likely to cause another kind of stroke.

The first task was restoring the aged adobe hacienda, somewhat neglected after being unoccupied for several years. H. M. Jaramillo built the house around 1890 in the same manner that his father and grandfather had used in previous generations. He made adobe bricks on the property, bonding them together with mud plaster for thick, sturdy walls. With help from neighbors he hoisted huge pine logs above the walls for the roof beams, or *vigas*, forming a flat surface that was layered with packed earth, like the floors inside.

Originally the home had three rooms, a kitchen with a wood stove and corner fireplace, a bedroom with another fireplace, and a *sala*, or salon. In the next couple of decades the Jaramillos added three other rooms, wood floors, and a pitched tin roof. When Arturo was a child, there were two bedrooms with fireplaces, a kitchen, a pantry, a workroom for tasks such as weaving and stringing chiles, and a *sala* that was cleaned weekly but just used on special occasions a few days a year. The kitchen served as the main living and dining area. The family usually went to bed at nightfall, lighting the kerosene lamps only for doing homework or other important jobs.

When Arturo and Florence acquired the house in 1963 they were determined to maintain its historic character. To make it into a restaurant, though, they had to bring in electricity, modern plumbing, and gas heating, none easy to introduce in a structure of solid adobe. They also had to replace many of the old floorboards, buckled with age, repair serious cracks in the ceiling, replaster the walls, add a portal for extra dining space, and move some major fixtures. They decorated the interior with family heirlooms and portraits, and filled the deep windowsills with potted geraniums and begonias, just as grandmother had done. Levi Jaramillo, a family member and noted craftsman, made the tables and chairs, using much of the discarded old wood.

The refurbishing took two years, but Arturo and Florence preserved the venerable hacienda for posterity and made it a memorial to the earthy architecture of the Spanish American frontier. In tribute to H. M. Jaramillo they adopted his initials as the logo of Rancho de Chimayó, enlarging the J, placing it in the center, and bordering the letters with the outlines of a New Mexico map.

Most people would have rested on their laurels after such a massive restoration effort. Not the Jaramillos. Two decades later they repeated the process on the home directly across the street from the Restaurante, converting it into a bed-and-breakfast inn, the Hacienda Rancho de Chimayó.

The projects were similar because the houses originally were identical, built at the same time by the same people. H. M. Jaramillo and his brother Epifanio worked together on the two places, located on adjoining plots of family land. The two men married sisters and moved them into the matching homes.

Again the refurbishing was painstaking in its attention to authenticity, though it encompassed such modern conveniences as private bathrooms and ceiling fans. The Jaramillos plastered the walls with the traditional mixture of clay, straw, and wood ash that Epifanio Jaramillo had used a century earlier. The old tin roof was rusted beyond repair, but they duplicated the rust color in the new metal covering. In the three guest rooms added to the four already in the house, the adobe walls were made as wide as the originals, though that thickness was no longer needed for insulation and increased the construction costs considerably.

In this restoration Arturo and Florence had some extra assistance. Laura returned home after graduation from Trinity University in San Antonio to contribute both manual labor and her special design talents to the inn. She decorated each room individually, carefully selecting period antiques and reproductions to create charming Victorian country milieus. After completing the project, she decided to stay and apply her business training to the management of the family enterprises, turning her back on options for a banking career in Texas.

Together the Jaramillos made the Hacienda Rancho de Chimayó as wonderful as the Restaurante Rancho de Chimayó. It's one of the coziest and most compelling places to stay in New Mexico, and just as affordable as the food across the street. The two establishments are natural twins, historic haciendas fulfilling a noble vision and helping to preserve a distinctive way of life.

STRUGGLES AND SUCCESSES

The Restaurante was a daring venture when it opened in the fall of 1965. People throughout northern New Mexico admired the concept, but few thought it would work. Bankers, government agencies, and suppliers refused to do business with the fledgling company.

The location was the main concern. Set in a secluded rural area off a major highway, the Restaurante required customers to go out of their way to eat—not a popular prospect in the heyday of TV dinners. Santa Fe represented the closest concentration of potential clients and it was over a half-hour away. Chimayó's reputation was religious rather than culinary and its visitors were more likely to be fasting than feasting.

The food also presented a challenge to many prospective guests. The Jaramillos served meals like those Arturo had as a child, using old family recipes. Many Hispanic New Mexicans cooked in a similar fashion at home, but few people considered it a respectable style for restaurant fare. Even in Santa Fe and Albuquerque at the time the closest most restaurants came to native cooking was the same kind of "Mexican" food that could also be found in Dallas and Los Angeles, derived primarily from the Sonora in northern Mexico.

Rancho de Chimayó proudly offered "New Mexican" meals based on local preparations and ingredients. As they would do at home, the cooks used chile in virtually every entree, making them much spicier than Sonoran dishes. They also served specialties of the area—*carne adovada*, *posole*, *sopaipillas*, and more—that were unusual to many non-Hispanic guests. Craig Claiborne, then the food critic of the *New York Times*, was among the early diners stunned by the differences. Raving about the New Mexican items, which he called the best "Mexican" fare in the area, he pronounced the menu extraordinary and imaginative.

Today such a review for a new restaurant might clog the phone lines with reservations. When the article appeared, though, in December, 1965, hardly anyone outside New York—including the Jaramillos—read the *Times* or knew Claiborne's name. After the governor of New Mexico happened across the story and gave the Jaramillos a copy, they had to contact friends in the East to find out who the writer was. All they could remember was an urbane tourist asking a lot of questions about the food.

Claiborne didn't lure crowds to the Restaurante and neither did anything else at first. For several years business was erratic and the bottom line bled. Florence had to take outside jobs—sometimes two at a time—to support the family and often the restaurant, too. At times her pay checks went into the pockets of employees, who remained unfailingly loyal despite many slow months and occasional late wages.

Once the lack of customers led to an incident that helped consolidate local support for the Restaurante, important to its eventual success. U.S. Department of Agriculture officials were scheduled to come for lunch, to discuss the possibility of government assistance. The Jaramillos wanted to give an impression of success but didn't have any other reservations. They invited dozens of relatives and friends for a free lunch and then fed them cheerfully after the officials canceled at the last minute. Though the cost of the meal seemed like another serious setback, it garnered a great deal of good will in the community.

It took ten years to get restaurant suppliers to deliver to Chimayó, so Florence had to handle much of the grocery shopping. Arturo grew some of the produce in the early years, and purchased as much as possible from local farmers, but most crops were still in the field during Rancho de Chimayó's busiest season, the summer, and weren't harvested until business dropped in the fall. Dan Jaramillo, now the manager of the Restaurante, remembers spending hours as a student employee unloading Florence's car, brimming with provisions after a shopping expedition to Santa Fe.

Eventually suppliers came to Chimayó and so did customers. A glowing review in *New Mexico Magazine* in 1970 was an early turning point, helping to establish a solid regional reputation. National recognition took a little longer, but was emerging as early as 1971, when the Time-Life series Foods of the World featured the Restaurante in *American Cooking: The Great West*.

James Beard, the noted authority on American regional cuisines, was the consultant for the book, which became the definitive guide of the decade for food editors and chefs.

By 1980 *Bon Appétit* columnists Jeff and Jinx Morgan were praying in print that they could convince their family to substitute a Rancho de Chimayó Christmas dinner for what they called the traditional turkey trot. Scores of other writers added their plaudits, everyone from Mimi Sheraton, Craig Claiborne's successor, to the roving champions of down-home American cooking, Jane and Michael Stern. In their popular book *Goodfood* the Sterns described a Restaurante meal as "a stunning spectrum of subtle and loud flavors." The electronic media joined the bandwagon later in the 1980s, when the Public Broadcasting Service highlighted the Restaurante in its distinguished documentary "Great Chefs of the Southwest."

The restaurant industry bestowed honors as well. Colleagues elected Florence to the National Restaurant Association board, making her the first New Mexican to serve in that position, and also named her the 1987 Restauranteur of the Year in the state. In 1988 a respected trade journal, *Nation's Restaurant News*, inducted Rancho de Chimayó into its 80-member Fine Dining Hall of Fame, placing it alongside other acclaimed establishments from Lutèce in New York to Chez Panisse in Berkeley.

The Jaramillos built a backroads hacienda into one of the most cherished restaurants in the United States. Their concept from the beginning was resolutely local in inspiration but grand in vision. Arturo and Florence in the early years, and Florence and Laura more recently, made Rancho de Chimayó a national treasure by helping to preserve the Spanish American heritage of a small, isolated town. Nobody will forget it.

America's Spanish Heritage

The first Spanish colonists in New Mexico settled a few miles west of Rancho de Chimayó, in the fertile Rio Grande Valley near San Juan Pueblo. Though it's a short drive today from the restaurant to the site of the village, it's a long, dramatic journey back in time. Spanish colonization in the United States is an epic frontier saga, too long ignored in the traditional textbooks, but basic to both a full appreciation of the American experience and an understanding of the way of life at Rancho de Chimayó.

The original settlers arrived in 1598, a year when the Pilgrim "Fathers" of Massachusetts were still children, and a decade before the English founded Jamestown, Virginia. They moved to the edges of the known world, extending the boundaries of the Spanish empire in the Americas to a remote, isolated territory that was a six-month journey from Mexico City, the capital of New Spain.

Spanish *conquistadores* and clerics had explored the region earlier. Two score years after Christopher Columbus raised the banner of the Spanish crown in the New World, and just a generation after Hernando Cortés subdued the Aztec empire in central Mexico, an adventuresome Franciscan friar led a small expedition into New Mexico in search of the legendary seven cities of gold. From a safe distance away Fray Marcos de Niza saw a Pueblo Indian mud village reflected in the intense southwestern sun and deceived himself into thinking that it was one of the world's most prodigal places.

In 1540 the royal viceroy in Mexico City sent an army under the command of Francisco Vásquez de Coronado to occupy the mythical cities. Coronado's knights in medieval armor were the first Europeans to see the Grand Canyon, the Continental Divide, and the vast American plains, but they failed to find gold, claiming far more land for Spain than mineral riches. Their most important discovery, at least in the eyes of the crown and the church, was thousands of Pueblo souls to save.

Coronado's expedition encountered some seventy Indian *pueblos*, or villages, concentrated most heavily in the Rio Grande Valley of northern New Mexico. None of the communities rivaled the Aztec capital of Tenochtitlan in grandeur, but they impressed the *conquistadores* in many ways. The Spaniards admired the sturdy adobe architecture, the skilled craftsmanship of the pottery and the weaving, the agricultural system that seemed to produce a bounty of corn, beans, squash, cotton, and tobacco. Again and again the troops commented that the Pueblos wore clothes and shoes, as if that particularly qualified them for Christianization.

Religion was the immediate dividing line between the two peoples and would remain so for many years. The Pueblos were as devout as the Spanish, but not in a way that a Castilian Catholic of that age could appreciate. When New Spain sent settlers to the distant region in 1598 the official purpose was the conversion and salvation of the Indians.

That mission dominated much of seventeenth-century New Mexico life. The early colonists still had lingering dreams of gold and silver, but those hopes faded in the first decade, a period of mistakes, hardships, and defections. The king of Spain was ready to abandon the province until some overly optimistic Franciscans claimed they were making significant progress with the Pueblos. The friars convinced the king to maintain the colony, and he ordered a new beginning at a new capital, which led to the founding of Santa Fe in 1610.

Some historians call the next 70 years the "Great Missionary Era." Some 250 Franciscans toiled among the Pueblos in that period, and the Spanish monarchy spent as much as $20 million in today's currency on churches, salaries, and other support costs. The crown made money in southern New Spain—now Mexico—but the pesos flowed the other way on the northern frontier.

Though the intent of the crusade was humanitarian, the Pueblos didn't view it that way. They had to provide the labor that sustained the missionary effort, erecting huge adobe churches, attending to the personal needs of the friars, even serving as *fiscales*, officers who assured the compulsory attendance of villagers at an endless round of religious services.

These demands on their time, coupled with tributes due to the civil authorities, angered the Pueblos, but not as much as another Spanish requirement. The Franciscans felt—quite rationally from their point of view—that anyone adopting Christianity should give up his or her former beliefs. The polytheistic Pueblos took a different attitude, equally reasonable to them, that the acceptance of new gods in no way discredited the old. They were happy to become Catholics as long as they could continue to practice their naturalistic religion as well. That was blatant heresy to Spaniards in the age of the Inquisition.

This conflict, aggravated by a severe drought and widespread famine, ultimately led to the Pueblo Revolt of 1680. The various Indian villages formed a rare alliance and drove the colonists from New Mexico for a dozen years. It was the most damaging rout the Spanish empire suffered in the Americas, inflicted by some of the most peaceful natives in New Spain.

The Revolt permanently altered colonial life in New Mexico. When the Spaniards returned from exile in 1692-93 their focus shifted away from missionary activities toward a broader effort at establishing a permanent base along the Rio Grande. The Franciscans continued to work among the Pueblos for another century, but the Indians learned to be more secretive about their religion—a practice they still continue—and the friars learned to look the other way. In secular realms the two peoples began to live in independent harmony, like distant neighbors, drawn together occasionally by trade and by mutual defense against raiding parties of Plains Indians.

Though the colony had always supported itself agriculturally, the cultivation of the land increasingly became more important than the cultivation of Christian souls. A different breed of new settlers came to the territory, people of the soil whose forebears were farmers and herders in Spain. Many of them were *Españoles-Mexicanos*, Spaniards who had been residing in Mexico City and its environs. Some were recent arrivals from the mother country and others were Creoles, pure Spaniards born in the New World. Among them were José Jaramillo Negrete, his wife Maria de Sotomayor, and their son Roque, the direct ancestors of the current Jaramillos of Chimayó.

LAND, WATER, AND BREAD

Roque Jaramillo and many of the *Españoles-Mexicanos* settled a full day's journey north of Santa Fe in the high valleys between the Jemez Mountains and the snowy peaks of the Sangre de Cristos. The awesome surroundings were sacred to the Pueblos, who attributed spiritual qualities to the land and all of nature. The new colonists didn't share that sense of the soil, but land meant much more to them than simple real estate. It was a source of life, a sustaining and enriching core of their existence, and its availability was a major lure of New Mexico for them.

The vast majority of individual holdings after 1700 were small farmsteads called *ranchos*, just adequate in size to support an extended family. In addition to this acreage, everyone had access to common lands for grazing sheep and goats. The *paisanos*, or country people, who spread gradually throughout northern New Mexico in the eighteenth century were hard-working, self-sufficient pioneers, much closer to Thomas Jefferson's agrarian ideal than were his fellow Virginia planters.

Water was a perennial problem in the semiarid climate, a resource as vital and nurturing as the land. The settlers brought irrigation practices from Spain, similar to the ditch technology some of the Pueblos were already using. They dammed rivers and mountain streams, and with crude, hand-made tools, dug networks of *acequias* (ditches) to divert water to their fields during the growing season.

The construction, maintenance, and use of the irrigation ditches was a complex communal responsibility. Farmers on the same system chose a *mayordomo de acequia* (steward) from among themselves to oversee a variety of regular joint tasks, such as dam repairs, the annual cleaning of the ditches, and blessings of the water by *santos*, images of saints.

Neighboring families worked together on many other tasks as well, including the building of homes. New Mexicans had no access to milled lumber until late in the nineteenth century, so they used age-old materials at hand for their houses. They literally lived in the earth, erecting walls of rock-hard adobe blocks made from mud dried in the sun. Their land provided the clay, sand, and straw they needed for the adobe and it produced shelters that were durable, fire resistant, impervious to arrows, and well insulated against the cold of the winters and the heat of the summers.

The colonists finished the walls, inside and out, with a heavy coat of mud plaster. It was applied by hand, usually by the women, and had to be renewed annually to keep wind and water from eroding the joints between the adobe blocks. The resulting surface was soft and undulating, organic in line and texture.

Men and their burros went to the mountains to get the pine logs used for the *vigas*, or roof beams. Working in groups, they hoisted the beams over the walls with ropes, creating a flat roof that was layered with dirt up to a foot thick. The floor inside was also packed earth, sprinkled with water when it was swept.

Most families lived, cooked, and slept in the same room, which always had a corner fireplace that provided the only heating and usually the only lighting in the evening. When sons got married they frequently added rooms for their families to the original home, producing compounds that sprawled across the property, sometimes around an enclosed central courtyard. Doors opened to the outside, but seldom into other rooms of the house. For warmth and security both, windows were small, set high in the walls, and heavily shuttered.

Only a few rich officials and *hidalgos* could afford to bring furnishings or even eating utensils up to the colony on the long trek from Mexico City. *Paisanos* slept on woolsacks or sheep pelts, wrapped in a locally-woven blanket. They didn't have chairs and they ate at simple, hand-hewn tables low to the ground. Their most prized possessions usually were carved chests, used for storage, and *trasteros*, or cupboards, which held food, pottery ware, and spoons carved in wood or fashioned from gourds.

Everyone raised most of their own food. They grew the Pueblo staples of corn, beans, and squash, along with chile, wheat, orchard fruits, grapes, and melons, all probably brought in by early settlers. The harvest was dried in the fall, preserving it for consumption during the year ahead. After the produce was stored, toward the approach of Christmas, a few domesticated animals were slaughtered. Their meat was dried into jerky strips that were usually pulverized and boiled before being eaten. Since markets were months away, the only imported food products were items that would keep indefinitely, such as coffee, sugar, chocolate, and spices.

Sheep were the most important domesticated animals, both for mutton and for wool. Goats provided some meat as well as milk and cheese. The typical farmer supplemented the family diet with wild game and fish, but wasn't a great hunter. Few people owned firearms, and most had to rely on traps and the bow and arrow.

Women cooked food in the same fireplace used for heating, in outdoor barbecue pits, and in outdoor beehive-shaped adobe ovens. Some communities had water-powered mills for grinding grain, but many housewives ground their corn on a *metate*, a stone slab, rubbing it with a smaller stone called a *mano*. The cornmeal was used primarily for tortillas, which were served in one way or another at most meals. Frequently the tortilla, like medieval trencher bread, was the plate and spoon as well as the fare, just dunked into a pot of beans or wrapped around bits of meat flavored with chile.

Such simple meals were common in the colonial period, but the cooking was more elaborate on major occasions. Food played a central role in all community events, from weddings to wakes. A number of times each year neighbors pooled their resources and the women prepared special dishes, ones that evolved over the years into the regional specialties served at Rancho de Chimayó today. Life was meager on the frontier in many ways, but as long as the pioneers had land, water, and their daily bread, they had ample reason to celebrate.

CELEBRATIONS OF LIFE

The celebrations in a colonist's life began with birth. New Mexicans viewed baptism as both a critical Christian ritual and a joyous occasion for a fiesta. The sacrament itself cleansed the infant of original sin—essential in case of early death—and the ceremonies surrounding it linked the child to the community.

Padrinos, or godparents, played an important role in baptism and throughout a person's life. Parents selected them at birth and they became the spiritual elders of the child, a second set of parents in effect and the ones who took over primary care if the natural mother and father died. It was an honor to serve as a *padrino* and some of the most affluent, respected couples had a dozen or more *ahijados*, or godchildren.

The *padrinos* often made the infant's baptismal robe—a long, lacy gown of white cotton—and they always took the child to the priest for the sacrament. When they returned from the church, they recited a formal verse to the parents, declaring the child blessed. The parents repeated the verse, sealing a special bond with the *padrinos*, who now became their cherished *compadres*, or co-parents, for life.

The fiesta followed and lasted the rest of the day. Relatives and friends came from miles around, slipping a coin to the mother as they greeted her. The mother and her neighbors had spent hours preparing food treats, mostly sweets such as *biscochitos* (anise-flavored cookies), small cakes, raisins, and candy. While musicians played lively versions of religious and folk tunes, the adults drank wine and, if space permitted, danced.

Weddings were equally ceremonious and even more festive. Parents and *padrinos* always had a strong voice in choosing mates and they were responsible for handling the protocol of an engagement. The father of the prospective groom, often accompanied by the godfather, visited the father of the desired bride and made a formal proposal, either orally or in writing. The parents of the girl were expected to consider the proposal carefully for a few weeks and make a formal response, either positive or *dando calabazas*, which literally means "giving the squash."

If the bride's parents accepted an offer, they set a date for the *prendorio*, or engagement party, when relatives of the young man and woman would gather in her home. After a period of polite conversation, the groom's father would ask to meet "the coveted jewel" they were seeking. The bride's father introduced his daughter, continuing to refer to her as "the coveted jewel." Sometimes, though not usually, it was the first time the young couple had seen each other. The two knelt before her godfather, who blessed their union by placing a rosary over each of their necks.

A wedding date was set for the near future, usually in a slack period on the agricultural calendar, and the festivities went on for days. The groom's family provided the food for the fiesta, plus a wedding gown and other pretty dresses for the bride, and her family prepared a series of special meals and hosted most of the events. Virtually everyone in the neighborhood attended the ceremony at the church, the reception afterwards, and the wedding dance at a community hall that night, which went on until the wee hours.

The only other celebrations as exuberant as weddings were connected with Christian holidays, particularly Christmas and the holy day of the local patron saint. Every chapel, every village, and almost every kind of endeavor had patrons. Each of these saints was identified with a particular day of the year, traditionally believed to be the date of their death and therefore their birthday in heaven. Communities and individual families commemorated a number of important saints on their holy days, but the happiest occasions were *funciones* in honor of the village patron.

Since there were few priests on the frontier, and they were mainly missionaries to the Pueblos, a *funcion* was one of the few times during the year when a Padre visited rural areas. Everyone donned their finest clothes and started the day at the church with a high mass. Following the service they formed a procession and carried a statue of the patron saint around the church, returning it to the sanctuary eventually with prayers that the patron would help provide bountiful rain and a good harvest in the year ahead.

Afterwards, one or more people selected at the previous *funcion* to serve as *mayordomos* of the event invited the participants to their homes for food and drink. Depending on circumstances and local customs, they offered a full meal or just sweet snacks. Activities in the afternoon varied by time and place, but there was always a carnival atmosphere, with music, games, races, gambling, and more, all leading up to a big dance at the end of the day.

Some *funciones* featured traditional miracle plays, though they were performed more commonly at Christmas. *Los Pastores* was one of the most popular of these old pageants, so revered in New Mexico that it sometimes replaced Christmas Eve mass in the church when a priest wasn't available. Roles in the play were often passed down in families over several generations and almost everyone in a community made some contribution to a presentation.

The *Pastores* story is simple, but it was full of dramatic intensity for the colonists. They identified personally with the main characters, a band of shepherds who journey to Bethlehem to greet the newborn King. Lucifer follows the shepherds, tempting them in various ways and almost succeeding until he is thwarted by the angel San Miguel and the birth of Christ. When the *pastores* arrive at the manger, they offer various gifts, usually items cherished in the area such as a lamb, woolen fleeces, and herbs. The poorest of the party, humble Bartolo, has nothing to present except a dance, which he does as a fellow shepherd accompanies him on the guitar.

Another play, *Las Posadas*, tells of Mary and Joseph's quest for shelter in Bethlehem. Every night on the nine days before Christmas the holy couple wander the village searching for a *posada*, or inn, that will lodge them. After repeated rejections, they are accepted into a home and are greeted by the neighborhood with Christmas carols and refreshments.

On *Noche Buena*, Christmas Eve, the colonists lighted piles of carefully stacked logs, *luminarias*, in front of their homes, symbolizing the fires of the Bethlehem shepherds. Adults huddled around the bonfires to visit, but children usually stayed indoors because this was the night of *los abuelos*, the ancestors' ghosts who wandered the village looking for wayward youngsters. The children had their moment the next morning, bounding outside at sunrise to go door-to-door among the neighbors to claim Christmas treats such as *biscochitos*, apples, and piñon nuts.

At home families seldom exchanged gifts, but Christmas day was the most important occasion of the year for sharing food. When possible the expansive spread included fresh meat, perhaps venison, wild turkey, or pork. Families always had plenty of beans, chile, *posole*, corn tamales, and *empanaditas*. All living generations of the family gathered for the day, observing the most joyful of Christian holidays with an abundance of their favorite flavors.

The Christmas feast and other celebrations were rare frills on the New Mexico frontier, but they enriched life and left a venerable legacy of Spanish customs in New Mexico.

THE LEGACY TODAY

With little warning and even less claim to justification, the U.S. Army marched into New Mexico in 1846 and seized the territory. At that point New Mexico and its sister province of California were a part of the recently founded nation of Mexico, which had won its independence from Spain a generation earlier. An expansionist American president, James K. Polk, started a war with Mexico as a pretext to conquer California and realize his country's "Manifest Destiny" of reaching from the Atlantic to the Pacific. Few people in Washington, D.C., considered New Mexico itself a prime prize, but it was on the way west and weakly defended.

On August 18, 1846, General Stephen W. Kearny raised the American flag over Santa Fe, severing New Mexico from its historical and cultural roots. It was the first of a century-long series of traumatic changes that would wrench the old colony into the modern world. The railroad wasn't far behind Kearny, and neither were land-hungry ranchers and shysters using English-language law to dispossess *paisanos*.

A cash economy gradually spread out of Santa Fe to the valley and mountain villages, undermining agricultural self-sufficiency and requiring new forms of labor. Land formerly held in common for sheepherding became National Forest land, and the authorities restricted grazing, for reasons they considered environmentally sound and villagers considered conspiratorial. Service in foreign wars, automobiles, radios, and televisions broadened horizons while eroding traditional values. Everything that happened seemed to threaten a way of life that had thrived for three centuries.

Much of the Spanish heritage has been lost, but under the circumstances the amazing thing is how much has survived. Few families can support themselves on their land now, but *acequias* still flow to fields all over northern

New Mexico and *mayordomos* supervise the maintenance of the ditches. Most residents of the area live in adobe homes that resemble those of the past, even if the floors are carpeted these days. They eat in chairs at an elevated table, but the staples of the diet are the same and the Christmas day family feast is similar. Many communities continue to honor their patron saint and still perform *Los Pastores* and *Las Posadas*.

The Spanish legacy, diluted but hardly dead, lives on in Chimayó and other colonial villages. It's a heritage that deserves understanding, appreciation, and preservation. Rancho de Chimayó plays a leading role in that effort, offering an experience of an American way of life too little known to most Americans.

The Spell of Chimayó

Chimayó sprawls across the upper end of a mountain valley the early Spaniards called La Cañada. At its highest point, near the site of Rancho de Chimayó, the valley rises to over 6,500 feet and sweeps downward from there to the Rio Grande, about ten miles away. The Rio Quemado flows into the town from the 13,000-foot Truchas Peaks to the northeast, and near the Restaurante joins another mountain stream, the Rio Santa Cruz, which cuts a winding path through the valley floor.

The landscape must have astounded the original settlers, just as it does first-time visitors today. The rugged Sangre de Cristos behind Chimayó abound with soaring forests and lush meadows, fed by winter snows and summer thunderstorms. The lowlands along the rivers are equally verdant, but serenely bucolic in contrast to the imposing summits. The foothills of the mountains, just above the valley, are another world again—arid sandstone cliffs, eroded and almost barren. The combination of environments, at once foreboding and exhilarating, exerts an eerie magnetism.

Manuel Jaramillo must have felt that lure when he established his *rancho* in Chimayó in the early eighteenth century, probably in the 1720s. Manuel was the son of Roque, who came to New Mexico with his parents in 1693. Only 11 at the time, Roque served as a soldier on the trek north from Mexico City. Later he married Manuel's mother, Petrona de Cardenas, and settled near the western end of La Cañada, not far from the Rio Grande.

Wanting land for his own family, Manuel moved east up the valley and chose a farm site on the present location of Rancho de Chimayó. It was a

Hermenegildo M. Jaramillo

Trinidad Jaramillo

sparsely populated area at the time, on the fringes of the frontier, probably as forlorn as it was alluring.

Chimayó grew slowly over the next half century. When Fray Francisco Atanasio Dominguez made an official tour of the New Mexico colony in 1776, there were 71 families in the village and a population of 376. The friar reported that some of the people lived on the Rio Santa Cruz and others were dispersed to the south, constituting together a "large settlement" compared to others outside Santa Fe. He also noted that the land was productive, the orchards were numerous, and the trout fishing was good in the river.

Sometime between Manuel Jaramillo's homesteading and the friar's visit, Chimayó residents erected a fortified town plaza. Until recently most authorities placed the construction of the Plaza del Cerro before the 1740s and assumed it was the original center of the town, basing their views primarily on research conducted in the 1950s. Local historian Dan Jaramillo, manager of the Restaurante Rancho de Chimayó, has refuted those conclusions lately.

THE TRUNK OF THE JARAMILLO FAMILY TREE

José Jaramillo Negrete-Maria de Sotomayor

Roque Jaramillo-Petrona de Cardenas

Manuel Jaramillo-Maria Medina

Miguel Jaramillo-Maria Felipa Martin

Manuel Jaramillo-Rosalia Trujillo

Anastacio Jaramillo-Casimira Martin

Hermenegildo M. Jaramillo-Trinidad Jaramillo

Matias Martinez-Leonardita Jaramillo

Arturo Jaramillo-Florence Poulin

Laura Ann Jaramillo

Researched by Dan Jaramillo, great-great-grandson of Miguel and Maria Jaramillo

In the process of writing the definitive Chimayó history, he uncovered fresh evidence that the plaza probably dates from the 1770s, a decade when Comanche Indians were constantly raiding New Mexico.

Severely deteriorated but still standing today near the junction of Highways 76 and 520, the Plaza del Cerro is one of the few surviving examples of a common form of colonial village defense. Spanish farmers liked to live on the land they tilled, in their scattered *ranchos*, but that made them a convenient target for Plains Indians, who posed a serious threat throughout the eighteenth century. Since the small army in Santa Fe was too distant to offer much protection, officials encouraged rural settlers to congregate in fortified towns.

The *rancheros* complied to the degree that the danger warranted. In Chimayó as in other towns, they built homes around a large plaza, with all windows and doors facing inward. Except for a narrow entrance, the exterior of the quadrangle was a solid adobe wall. The plan provided a good measure of safety, though the farmers sometimes had to call on other resources as well. According to one old story, once when Comanches occupied the village of Truchas, just north of Chimayó, the residents sneaked back to their homes at night and stuffed strings of chile down smoking chimneys, which they then sealed. The Indians fled, victims of one of history's first tear gas attacks.

Among the homes on the Plaza del Cerro is an old chapel, the Oratorio de San Buenaventura, locally venerated but no longer used for religious services. Many people assume it dates back to the construction of the plaza itself, making it the first chapel in Chimayó. Dan Jaramillo's research demonstrates differently. He has found a nineteenth-century family will that places the origins of the Oratorio in the 1820s or 1830s, after the founding of El Santuario de Nuestro Señor de Esquípulas.

The Santuario is the most famous church in the Southwest. Many others are grander, some are equally revered, but none compare in spiritual reputation or intensity. Long before anyone thought of coming to Chimayó to eat, the small chapel made the town a place of pilgrimage.

A PLACE OF PILGRIMAGE

Manuel Jaramillo may have grazed sheep a short walk from his homestead at a spot called El Potrero, Spanish for "pasture land." The earth his flock would have treaded probably was sacred to the Pueblos from centuries before and certainly would become holy to later generations of New Mexicans. At least from the early 1800s up to the present, and possibly for as long as a thousand years, people have walked great distances to the pasture on religious missions of prayer, healing, and thanksgiving.

The Santuario is the destination of these pilgrims today, but in the distant past Indians may have been seeking mud with curative powers from a hot spring or pool near the site of the church. Several contemporary Pueblos, including the famous potter Maria Martinez, have said the spot was an ancient shrine. According to these accounts the mud derived its therapeutic properties from the time when the twin war gods tracked and killed a giant that was devouring children. As the monster died, the earth spewed fire and smoke through ponds at El Potrero and a couple of other places, creating pools of healing mud.

Perhaps Pueblo visits to this shrine in the colonial period encouraged the Spaniards to wonder about the soil. All we know for sure is that a prominent Chimayó citizen, Bernardo Abeyta, had a religious experience around 1810 that convinced him and his neighbors that they had miraculous earth at El Potrero. Accounts of what happened vary substantially, but according to Abeyta's granddaughter, he discovered a crucifix of Our Lord of Esquípulas in a hole in the ground. Three times he took the crucifix to the church in nearby Santa Cruz, but on each occasion it disappeared from there and returned to the spot where it was originally discovered.

Abeyta knew then that the dirt in the hole was as blessed as the crucifix, because in Central America Our Lord of Esquípulas was associated with the healing powers of earth and hot springs. Abeyta erected a *hermita*, or small shelter, over the holy ground and obtained permission to build a private chapel alongside. He completed the Santuario in 1816, with the *hermita* attached.

Some of the first pilgrims to the church were members of the Cofradía de Nuestro Padre Jesús Nazareno, better known as the Penitente Brotherhood. Abeyta was an early leader and perhaps one of the creators of the brotherhood, which became a major religious force in New Mexico in the nineteenth and early twentieth centuries. Some people today sensationalize the Penitentes, focusing on their flagellation rites during Holy Week, when they relived the agonies of the crucifixion. That was only one aspect of their passionate faith, however. The complex fraternity was active in community affairs year-round, and its impact was clearly beneficial and humane in places like Chimayó.

Abeyta's granddaughter said he discovered the miraculous crucifix during Lenten penances with the Penitentes. That may have helped to attract his brothers to the Santuario; certainly his position in the organization did. They in turn spread the word about the church and the blessed earth, probably contributing significantly to the numbers of early pilgrims. By the time Abeyta died in 1856 the Santuario was renowned throughout northern New Mexico.

The founder would have been surprised, though, about a change that occurred in the following decades. The chapel added a statue of the Santo Niño de Atocha to its religious icons, partially at least to match a similar *santo* drawing visitors to a new neighboring church. The Santo Niño was one of the most popular saints in the frontier colony, beloved for running errands of mercy at night, constantly wearing out his shoes. He was also the patron saint of pilgrims and travelers, which made him a particular favorite at the Santuario. Over time the Santo Niño's spiritual association with the healing powers of the earth came to surpass that of the crucifix of Our Lord of Esquípulas. The transference was so complete that at this point there is even some doubt about which of the two crucifixes in the church is the original.

Thousands of people continue to come to the Santuario annually, especially during Holy Week, when many make the journey on foot from miles around. A few still bring shoes for the Santo Niño, to replace his worn ones, and most still gather a little of the blessed earth from the hole under Abeyta's *hermita*.

The chapel has changed little in appearance since the early nineteenth century. The adobe facade, including the two distinctive bell towers, has withstood time, aided now by a stucco finish. Benches and a floor were added to the interior, but the altar screen, *retablos* (paintings on flat boards), and *bultos* (carved statues) all date from the church's early decades.

The religious art is intensely expressive, as passionate as you would expect of a Penitente patron. All of it was made in or near Chimayó by untrained folk artists working within village craft traditions.

VILLAGE CRAFTS

In the period when the Santuario was built there may have been more *retablos* and *bultos* in New Mexico than people. Churches brimmed with these *santos* and every home had at least a few. The sacred images played a vital role in colonial religion, serving as intermediaries with God during a time when priests were scarce, and providing models of saintly living and suffering that inspired personal identification.

The creators of the *santos* were *santeros*, painters and sculptors who worked with simple tools and organic materials from the area. A few of the more skilled plied their craft as a trade, but many were occasional artisans, carpenters elaborating on their skills with wood, or farmers filling idle hours in the winter with devotional work.

The *santeros* developed a distinctive New Mexican style by 1750. They turned away from the representational conventions of Spanish and Mexican art toward a more poignant primitive symbolism. At the same time they began replacing Old World characterizations of their subjects with bold local interpretations. Their saints were portrayed in the ways they were revered on the frontier, taking on many of the features and the dress of the colonists.

Chimayó had a number of part-time *santeros* over the years, but little is known about them. Many of the *santos* in the town, including those at the Santuario, probably were made in the neighboring village of Cordova, a few miles away. Cordova established an early reputation for its work some 200 years ago and has maintained it since.

Cordova's leading *santero* in the nineteenth century was José Rafael Aragon, one of the most prolific and perhaps the most skilled of all the colonial folk artists. A carpenter who served as his assistant, José Nasario Lopez, taught wood-working techniques to his son, José Dolores Lopez, a talented carver "discovered" and promoted in the early twentieth century by members of the Santa Fe art colony.

George Lopez, José Dolores' son, attained broader recognition for the same skill. In the 1980s the National Endowment for the Arts honored him as a national treasure. Members of George's family and other Cordova artisans continue to carry on the carving tradition, and several sell graceful, unpainted pieces out of their homes, ten minutes by car from Rancho de Chimayó.

Even closer to the restaurant are several shops that specialize in Chimayó's own special craft, weaving. The town is so identified with proficiency at the loom that all New Mexico blankets were once called "Chimayós," regardless of where they were woven. Collectors today prefer the term "Rio Grande" to describe the regional Spanish style, but Chimayó remains the weaving center of the state, as it has been for generations.

The earliest Spanish settlers in New Mexico brought sheep with them and a solid understanding of European weaving traditions. The Pueblos were already making cotton cloth on vertical looms, but the colonists introduced horizontal looms and wool, which was warmer for clothing and more resistant to flame. Following customs of the Old World, men sheared the sheep and carded the wool, while women spun the yarn with a *malacate*, or spindle. They learned to collect *amole*, or yucca root, to wash the lanolin from the yarn, and other native plants to use for dyes. Normally men did the actual weaving, usually in the winter when their fields and flocks needed less attention.

They wove several kinds of fabric for different purposes, but blankets were the most important product, serving as a coat during the day and as a sleeping bag at night. Since they wore an outer garment many months of the year, blankets became a source of pride, demonstrating the quality of a family's wool, yarn, and design skills.

Probably a number of Chimayó's original settlers were weavers, but the first we know about was Nicolás Gabriel Ortega, born about 1729, who founded a dynasty of artisans. Every generation of his direct descendants up to the present included at least one weaver, usually more, and some of them intermarried with another family of masters, the Trujillos, who date back in Chimayó to 1759.

The Ortegas, Trujillos, and other villagers continued making blankets throughout the nineteenth century, when the craft was gradually abandoned in most of New Mexico because of the increasing availability of cheap, factory-made substitutes from the East. Over time some of the artisans began using commercial yarn, already dyed, but fathers still passed down their looms and techniques to their sons. A clearly identifiable local style emerged, featuring a solid, bold background color, abstract diamond or thunderbird motifs in the center, bands of stripes on the edges, and a strong sense of symmetry.

At the turn of the twentieth century most of the local weaving was still done for personal use, but that changed quickly in the following decades as the village shifted to a cash economy. The railroad first and then automobiles brought more and more tourists to New Mexico and they provided an eager market for blankets and other products. Enterprising weavers became merchants, selling "Chimayós" along the old Route 66, in Santa Fe, and eventually in their own shops in the town itself.

Severo Jaramillo was one of the early entrepreneurs. Born in 1891, he married Teresita Trujillo and both became weavers. Their farm alone wouldn't support them, so Severo opened a small grocery and filling station, now closed. He had his huge, handmade loom in the store and between customers he made blankets, which he sold to gas-buying travelers.

Jacobo and Isabel Trujillo set up shop in their home about the same period, next to their orchards alongside Highway 76. Jacobo was one of the most talented craftsmen of his day and frequently served as a teacher and mentor to others, including his son Irvin, who left an engineering career to open Centinela Traditional Arts with his father in 1983. They named the shop for its location on the old family homestead, the spot where in previous centuries sentinels guarded Chimayó from Indian raids. Irvin and his wife Lisa, both gifted weavers, run the gallery today.

Nicacio and Virginia Ortega founded the largest and best-known business. They became a "Traficador en Serape" in 1900 and built the current Ortega's Weaving Shop in 1946 with their sons David, José Ramon, and Ricardo. When Nicacio died in 1964, José Ramon and David took over the shop. In recent years David managed the shop with the assistance of his wife Jeanine, until her death in 1991, and of their sons Andrew and Robert. David, Andrew, and Robert continue to run the shop. At the town's most prominent intersection, the junction of Highways 76 and 520, Ortega's sells blankets, rugs, jackets, place mats, and other items made by scores of local artisans, mostly people supplementing the family income with part-time work.

These and similar businesses help preserve an important aspect of the Chimayó heritage. The craft of weaving in the town has changed in a number of ways over time, but it's still a source of pride and a tangible connection to the pastoral past.

THE CHERISHED CHILE

Along with its blankets and its Santuario, Chimayó has long been known for its red chile. The reputation goes back almost a century and a half, when local farmers first began bartering their produce with Spanish settlers in the San Luis Valley of southern Colorado.

Before then chile was just one of many crops, well suited to the soil, but not more important than the others for agricultural self-sufficiency. Like all of the fall harvest, it was dried for preservation, in this case on long strings, or *ristras*. The colonists hung the fiery red *ristras* from the roofs of their homes, drying them in the sun, as Rancho de Chimayó still does today.

The early farmers grew at least a little of everything they could, but beans, wheat, and potatoes didn't do as well as chile and orchard fruits. The opposite was the case in the San Luis Valley, nearly a hundred miles north. By the middle of the nineteenth century, within a few decades of Spanish expansion into Colorado, the two areas discovered their reciprocal differences and began trading.

Shortly after the harvest, Chimayó chile growers loaded up covered wagons with produce and blankets and took off on the long journey. They traveled in a group, usually a half dozen wagons, sometimes twice that many. The annual caravans continued until World War I, even after easier transportation became available in the 1880s on the Chile Line, the railroad spur between Santa Fe and Antonito, Colorado.

The San Luis residents bartered a lot in goods for the cherished chiles. They would exchange 140 pounds of wheat or 16 pounds of beans for two of the scarlet *ristras*. Their potatoes fetched less, only a *ristra* and a half for a full sack.

Chimayó's Colorado connection dwindled as both areas shifted to a cash economy, but chile retained its importance locally. It became the dominant money crop and brought good prices until the Great Depression of the 1930s, when a *ristra* plunged in value from $1 to 35 cents. Though every family in town at the time was still growing most of their own food, they devoted a third of the land under cultivation to chile, producing ample surplus to market.

The Depression hit hard in Chimayó and the old agricultural system wasn't up to the strain. The population had grown beyond the ability of the land to support it, and the long-tilled soil was losing some of its fertility. Fewer families could make a living as farmers and that became increasingly so in the decades beyond. Today many residents continue to grow their favorite crops, but it's usually a secondary source of income rather than the primary occupation.

As Chimayó chile was declining in commercial importance, it was rising in culinary stature, due in large measure to Rancho de Chimayó. The restaurant was one of the first anywhere to employ chile some way in virtually every main dish, and the kitchen has always featured the local product when it was available in sufficient supply. It's a business built on chile in many respects, and it has gradually inherited much of chile's role in sustaining the Chimayó economy.

Though Chimayó has changed considerably over its 300-year history, it has done so less than most towns its age. If Manuel Jaramillo, Nicolás Gabriel Ortega, and Bernardo Abeyta came back today, they would readily recognize the village as their own. Abeyta would find the Santuario much the same and would be pleased about the number of pilgrims still visiting. Ortega would appreciate the contemporary weaving. Jaramillo would like the look of the Rancho de Chimayó on his land, and would enjoy the chile, close in taste to his own. Despite cars, televisions, and other modern intrusions, the three would feel at home, comfortable with Chimayó's continuing traditions.

THE FOOD
&
ITS PREPARATION

An Evolving Tradition

JOANNA ROY

Cooking Chimayó Style at Home

The food served at Rancho de Chimayó is a piquant expression of a living heritage, steeped in tradition, but it is not historic cookery frozen in the colonial past. Though the main ingredients haven't changed much in 300 years, the family recipes used at the restaurant have evolved substantially over the centuries. As generation after generation passed on its favorite dishes, imaginative cooks introduced individual interpretations shaped by the availability of ingredients, trends of the day, and personal taste preferences.

Most Rancho de Chimayó recipes are inspired by the fare prepared for family and friends on special occasions during Arturo Jaramillo's youth in the 1930s and '40s. Arturo's grandparents—who raised him in that period in the *casa* that is now the Restaurante—would love the food and take pride in the joy with which their family legacy is shared. The Jaramillos have added new dishes to the menu, though, and have made some contemporary modifications, such as the substitution of canola oil for lard. The kitchen respects the essence of the old traditions without being bound by old-fashioned prescriptions.

The recipes presented in the cookbook will allow anyone to duplicate Rancho de Chimayó fare at its finest, in meticulous detail, but you don't have to be slavish to the specifics to create wonderful New Mexican dishes true to their roots. Even the cooks at the restaurant occasionally vary seasonings according to their own individual feel for the ingredients.

Try your own variations and combinations. If you love cilantro but can't abide oregano, adjust the quantities to suit your taste. Substituting *queso de*

cabra (fresh goat cheese) in a cheese enchilada will give a more pungent flavor that both emulates the past and aligns the dish with contemporary Southwestern cooking. Modifications are a part of a living heritage and you, too, can participate in an evolving food tradition.

USING THIS BOOK

The recipes are organized by their usual placement in restaurant meals, but you can rearrange them according to your desires. A serving of two *flautas*, or of miniature tamales, can make a fine appetizer. Likewise, a Burrell tortilla is a great lunch entree.

Serving sizes are generous, characteristic of the Jaramillos' desire to give patrons more than their money's worth. Because the restaurant's cooking is hearty, many people assume it is unhealthy. Chile, beans, and corn, though, provide a fine balance of vitamins, protein, and carbohydrates. Moderation is the key to some of the dishes. A cardiologist might wince at a patient's nightly consumption of *carne adovada*, *carne asada*, or flan, but be unconcerned with an occasional indulgence.

Salt is present in most recipes, but in modest quantities. If you prefer, eliminate it altogether. In spicy recipes in particular, you may not notice its absence.

Exercise caution in dealing with raw eggs and chicken. The disturbing incidences of salmonella food poisoning require more careful handling and thorough cooking than has been traditionally called for. Avoid cutting poultry on a wood cutting board in favor of one with a non-porous surface that can be washed in hot soapy water. Remember while handling eggs or chicken to wash every utensil and surface that you have touched with more hot, soapy water, and then be sure to wash your hands well too. Layering newspaper on the work surface and using paper towels can help speed the cleanup. Safety experts now recommend that not only chicken, but egg preparations and dishes too, be cooked through. Never leave egg and chicken dishes at room temperature for longer than it takes to serve them.

Temperatures are given in Fahrenheit measurements.

For anyone unfamiliar with chiles or other ingredients used in some of the recipes, flip to the concluding chapter, New Mexico Products and Mail-Order Sources, which gives background details, possible substitutions, and purchasing information.

A cookbook based on the recipes of a restaurant nestled in a valley above 6,500 feet can't ignore the differences that occur in cooking at high and low altitudes. Most of the preparations are not so precise or temperamental that much, if any, change is needed. In the few dishes where the altitude does alter the cooking time substantially or otherwise affects the food's preparation, high altitude instructions accompany the standard recipe, written for readers living at lower altitudes.

CONTEMPORARY EQUIPMENT FOR COOKING STEEPED IN THE PAST

Little specialized equipment is required to prepare Rancho de Chimayó's recipes. The restaurant kitchen varies from a home kitchen mostly in the amount of equipment. Its 50-gallon bean cooker and two vats for deep-frying will be unnecessary unless you too plan to serve up to 1,000 people a day.

The only recipes that are substantially simplified by unusual (but inexpensive) equipment are those for corn and flour tortillas. To make corn tortillas of uniform thickness and shape, a tortilla press is almost essential unless you have years to perfect a hand technique. Flour tortillas can be prepared with a rolling pin, but if you plan to serve the homemade variety frequently, a narrower tortilla roller will speed the work. Tortilla presses and rollers can be ordered if you can't find them locally. See the concluding chapter, New Mexico Products and Mail-Order Sources.

The recipes assume that prospective cooks have a basic array of pots and pans and other food preparation utensils. Some late twentieth-century innovations in kitchen equipment and appliances can speed or simplify procedures, but they are not essential in most respects.

A crockpot, *the* 1970s wedding present, may be hidden away in your kitchen pantry. Its slow heat makes pork for tamales more tender than conventional oven baking, and also is great for warming pre-steamed tamales, holding them for several hours without drying out. Similarly, a crockpot is useful for warming and holding tortillas before serving time.

The blender comes in handy for some of the drinks, but it isn't necessary to the success of any. A cocktail shaker or lidded jar and a strong pair of arms can suffice. The one recipe that realistically requires a blender is *carne adovada*, where it makes quick work of puréeing the chile sauce to the proper consistency.

If you own a food processor, you likely are well aware of its abilities to speed the chopping of vegetables and the grating of cheese, helpful in such recipes as *pico de gallo* or Burrell tortillas. Don't overlook it for the major task of grating the zucchini in zucchini–green chile tamales. The plastic dough blade is great for shredding meat, eliminating the need to do that by hand for the pork tamale filling. The only use of the processor we strongly discourage is for the making of *sopaipilla* dough, still produced by hand at the restaurant.

Rancho de Chimayó owns a microwave, but doesn't cook in it. There are a few tasks, though, that a microwave can assist. Using a medium or medium-high setting, the oven melts cheese well, making it useful in dishes like nachos, Burrell tortillas, cheese enchiladas, or other cheese-topped recipes. Be careful not to cook these dishes beyond the cheese's melting point unless you're trying to make a patch for a tire. A microwave also bakes potatoes for the first step of fried potatoes in a matter of minutes, rather than an hour, and is good for reheating pre-steamed tamales or warming tortillas when the food is covered in plastic wrap.

When Rancho de Chimayó opened in 1965, many homes had deep-fat fryers. The typical lack of the appliance today makes deep frying a little awkward. High-sided, heavy skillets do the job but require large quantities of oil. Since the fried dishes often require high heat, the oil breaks down quickly and generally can't be reused. To save on oil, the Jaramillos recommend a wok. Obviously non-traditional, it nevertheless accomplishes the job with efficiency.

If you discover other ways to speed or simplify recipes, use them. The preparation of Rancho de Chimayó's food should be a labor of love rather than just a labor.

PLANNING YOUR TIME

Unlike Rancho de Chimayó, busy home cooks don't have an eager kitchen staff to help prepare and orchestrate meals. A handful of the restaurant recipes require lengthy preparation or cooking times and a few more need some last-minute attention. Other dishes require the assembling of several recipes.

Don't be daunted. The cooking looks more complicated than it really is. Remember that the food originated in the home. Many recipes can be made well in advance of meal time; the instructions indicate when this is the case. We note the dishes that freeze well, and each of these can be portioned into container sizes that suit your needs. A stash of pinto beans in the freezer is infinitely more appealing than having to rely on mushy canned beans when you're in a hurry.

All dishes that flourish in the freezer can be made in large batches for multiple meals. It's no harder to watch a pot of beans or *posole* that serves twelve than to tend a smaller pot serving six. Tamales are another good example, though making them in quantity is tedious work for one cook. Do like they do in Chimayó and enlist the aid of relatives or friends. Even when doubling the recipe, the tamales can be completed in less than half the time usually required if you have help.

Recipes for flour and corn tortillas are provided for authenticity, but even the restaurant no longer makes its own. The process is very time consuming and there are excellent sources for tortillas in northern New Mexico. Try your own if you're curious or don't have a superior source. The freshness of the resulting breads is reward in itself, especially if you plan to eat them unadorned.

Always make your own chile sauces and salsa at home, even if your time or patience is limited. You may think you can buy a reasonable ready-made substitute, but your own preparations will harmonize best with the dishes they flavor.

With a little imagination and advance planning, you'll discover that it's simple to make all kinds of different dishes with reasonable speed and without hiring your own kitchen staff.

CORE PREPARATIONS
AND COMBINATIONS

About a dozen of the book's recipes have multiple uses in different dishes and half of these form the core of the restaurant's cooking. The red and green chile sauces, in particular, star in every kind of dish other than drinks and desserts. The following list indicates the ways Rancho de Chimayó uses and combines various key recipes.

RED AND/OR GREEN CHILE SAUCES: Burrell Tortilla, Tamales, Enchiladas, Torta de Huevo con Chile y Carne, Burritos, Sopaipillas Rellenas, Carne Asada, Huevos Rancheros, Bistec Solomillo, Pollo Al Estilo Chimayó, Fried Potatoes, Torta de Huevo Tradicional

TOMATO SALSA: Tacos, Flautas, Tostadas

CHILE CON QUESO: Tostadas, Pollo Al Estilo Chimayó

PICO DE GALLO: Tostadas, Fajitas

CARNE ADOVADA: Carne Adovada, Burrito Al Estilo Madril

PINTO BEANS: "Refried" Beans, Tacos, Flautas, Burritos

SOPAIPILLAS: Sopaipillas Rellenas, Sopaipillas with Cinnamon and Sugar, Sopaipilla Cream Puffs

FLOUR TORTILLAS: Burrell Tortilla, Burritos, Fajitas

CORN TORTILLAS: Tostadas, Flautas, Enchiladas, Tacos, Huevos Rancheros

TOSTADAS: Tomato Salsa, Guacamole, Chile con Queso, Nachos, Pico de Gallo

NATILLAS: Sopaipilla Cream Puffs

BEBIDAS
Beverages

The recipes included here are for alcohol-based concoctions, all delicious but also quite strong. Please drink responsibly and encourage your guests to do the same. Do not drink and drive. For designated drivers or anyone who just prefers to avoid alcohol, apple cider, iced tea, and soda are fine accompaniments to a New Mexican meal.

Chimayó Cocktail

When the Restaurante first opened, the Jaramillos looked for ways to popularize Chimayó's apple cider, hoping to make its commercial production more viable for area farmers. After weeks of experimentation they hit upon the Chimayó Cocktail, a potent concoction that is now the restaurant's signature drink and its most requested recipe.

Serves 1

1½ ounces (1½ jiggers) Cuervo Gold or other high-quality gold tequila
1 ounce apple cider, preferably unfiltered
¼ ounce lemon juice
¼ ounce crème de cassis
1 slice unpeeled apple

Half fill an 8-ounce glass with ice cubes. Pour all of the ingredients over the ice and stir to blend. Garnish the rim with the apple slice and serve.

For a lighter summer punch, prepare the cocktail as described, multiplying by the number of servings desired. Add sparkling water in a quantity equal to the cocktail mixture. For an attractive party presentation, serve in a punch bowl over ice with floating slices of apple.

Chimayó's apples were plentiful until a disastrous 1971 freeze wiped out much of the orchard industry. Two of the oldest trees survived the calamity, continuing to flourish on the old town plaza. Spanish settlers planted the pair from seeds they brought with them in the eighteenth century.

Margarita

This is not the drink for those who think the margarita should be a syrupy limeade cooler, a popular 1980s aberration. The Rancho de Chimayó's tart-sweet blend is truer to the drink's classic proportions. Bars on both sides of the Rio Grande take credit for the margarita's original formulation, which probably dates to the 1930s. Whatever the drink's heritage, the Restaurante's version is the perfect antidote for the heat of summer days or spicy food. Chris Barela, an early customer, first suggested the switch from the traditional lime juice to lemon. It caught on quickly with the staff, and with the restaurant's other patrons.

Serves 1

Salt
Lemon wedge
1½ ounces (1½ jiggers) Cuervo
   Gold or other high-quality gold
   tequila

1 ounce triple sec
¾ ounce lemon juice

Place a thin layer of salt onto a saucer. Rub the rim of an 8-ounce glass with the lemon wedge and immediately dip the rim into the salt. Set aside. (Omit this step if you prefer your margarita *sin sal*, without salt.)

Pour the tequila, triple sec, and lemon juice into a cocktail shaker or lidded jar, add several ice cubes, and shake to blend. Pour into the prepared glass and serve.

Margaritas go well with parties and fiestas. Without a bartender at home to mix every drink to order, you may want to make a larger quantity shortly before serving time. The recipe can be multiplied by the number of drinks desired. Squeeze lemons into a bowl until you've measured the quantity of juice required. Pour the juice and the adjusted amounts of tequila and triple sec into a large lidded jar, cover, and set aside. Just before serving time, salt the rims of all the glasses. Add 2 to 3 ice cubes per serving to the jar and shake vigorously. Pour into the prepared glasses and serve.

Grand Gold Margarita

For an important celebration, try a more lavish twist on the old favorite.

Serves 1

Salt
Lemon wedge
1½ ounces (1½ jiggers) Cuervo
    1800, Herradura Gold, or other
    premium gold tequila

1 ounce Grand Marnier
¾ ounce lemon juice

Place a thin layer of salt onto a saucer. Rub the rim of an 8-ounce glass with the lemon wedge and immediately dip the rim into the salt. Set aside. (Omit this step if you prefer your margarita *sin sal*, without salt.)

    Pour the tequila, Grand Marnier, and lemon juice into a cocktail shaker or lidded jar, add several ice cubes, and shake to blend. Pour into the prepared glass and serve.

Blue Margarita

When Rancho de Chimayó opened in 1965, the "Blue Hawaiian" was a popular tropical drink, made with the then exotic, azure-colored Curaçao liqueur. Bartender John Romero helped concoct a more New Mexican libation with the same ingredient. The Curaçao's orange flavoring is similar to triple sec.

Serves 1

Salt
Lemon wedge
1½ ounces (1½ jiggers) Cuervo
    Gold or other high-quality gold
    tequila

1 ounce blue Curaçao
¾ ounce lemon juice

Place a thin layer of salt onto a saucer. Rub the rim of an 8-ounce glass with the lemon wedge and immediately dip the rim into the salt. Set aside. (Omit this step if you prefer your margarita *sin sal*, without salt.)

    Pour the tequila, Curaçao, and lemon juice into a cocktail shaker or lidded jar, add several ice cubes, and shake to blend. Pour into the prepared glass and serve.

Gonzalo Special

Vacations don't come easily when you a run a restaurant. For many years the Jaramillos headed south just across the border to Juarez when they could get away for a couple of days' respite. The Hotel Camino Real's bartender, Señor Gonzalo, made a potent elixir like this for torrid days spent languidly by the pool. The Camino Real and Señor Gonzalo are only memories now, but the spirit of those family getaways lives on when you sip a Gonzalo Special.

Serves 1

1½ ounces vodka
1½ ounces light rum
1½ ounces orange juice

1 ounce pineapple juice
½ ounce grenadine

Fill a tall 10- to 12-ounce glass with ice cubes. Pour the ingredients over the ice. Add a straw and serve immediately.

Hot Mulled Wine

Skiers returning to Santa Fe after a day on the slopes at Taos Ski Valley often stop at the restaurant's cantina for a warming drink in front of a blazing fire. The wine works well for entertaining a group of friends on a chilly evening.

Serves 12

1 liter red wine
Orange
8 to 12 cloves
6 to 8 cinnamon sticks

2 to 3 whole nutmegs, their
    surfaces grated slightly
Additional cinnamon sticks,
    optional, for garnish

Pour the wine into a large non-reactive saucepan or a stockpot.

Slice the orange in half and stud the skin of each piece with an equal number of cloves. Place the orange halves in the wine. Add the cinnamon and the nutmegs to the mixture.

Simmer over very low heat for 30 minutes. Do not boil. Discard the spices. Serve steaming, ladled into mugs or coffee cups. Garnish with additional cinnamon sticks, if desired.

Cidre Caliente con Tuaca

For a delicious non-alcoholic alternative, briefly heat the cider with a vanilla bean and a generous slice of orange peel (white pith removed) in a small saucepan. Remove the cider from the heat and let it steep for 30 minutes. Strain out the orange peel and the vanilla bean—the bean can be rinsed and dried for a later use—and gently reheat. Serve warm, topped with cinnamon and whipped cream as described.

Popular New Mexico musicians stroll through the cantina and restaurant, serenading appreciative diners and adding to the considerable local character. Over the years, the best-known and best-loved performers have been David Salazar, the late Jacki McCarty, and Genoveva Chavez y El Trio Melódico. The trio still appears regularly, as they have for more than 20 years.

Tuaca is an Italian liqueur perfumed with vanilla and a hint of orange. When the Jaramillos were looking for drinks that could feature Chimayó's apple cider, they discovered a version of this recipe supplied by the producers of Tuaca. The aromatic cross-cultural beverage can replace dessert.

Serves 1

2 ounces (2 jiggers) Tuaca liqueur
6 ounces apple cider, heated

Cinnamon to taste
Whipped cream

Measure the Tuaca into an 8-ounce mug and add the hot cider. Sprinkle cinnamon generously over the cider. Mound whipped cream on top of the liquid and garnish with another sprinkling of cinnamon. Add a straw and serve immediately.

Café Mexicano

Serves 1

1 ounce (1 jigger) Cuervo Gold or
   other high-quality gold tequila
¼ ounce Kahlúa

6 ounces freshly-brewed coffee
Whipped cream
Lemon zest

Measure the tequila and Kahlúa into an 8-ounce mug and add the coffee. Top with whipped cream and lemon zest. Serve piping hot.

Café Español

Serves 1

¾ ounce (¾ jigger) Kahlúa   6 ounces freshly-brewed coffee
¾ ounce brandy   Whipped cream

Measure the Kahlúa and brandy into an 8-ounce mug and add the coffee. Top with whipped cream. Serve piping hot.

NOTES ON MEXICAN BEERS

Though there are wines that can stand up to the assertively seasoned food at Rancho de Chimayó—such as some fumé blancs, Gewürztraminers, and zinfandels—Mexican beer is a more popular choice and usually a better match. Developed originally by German immigrants a century ago, Mexican breweries produce some of the best beers in the world. Most of the ones served at the restaurant are relatively light in body and taste, if not in calorie count. Carta Blanca, Tecate, and Corona are the closest to American lagers, though they are bolder in flavor. The most distinctive and robust options are Dos Equis, a malty brew, and Bohemia, a well-balanced but hearty beer with a hops edge.

Distributors throughout the United States now carry these beers. In most areas it should be easy to find one or more to accompany a home-cooked New Mexican meal.

Tomato Salsa

Chimayó's short, dry summers and cool nights were never conducive to tomato growing, but the canned variety became common in northern New Mexico with the advent of the railroad. Now fresh tomatoes are readily available, but the quality fluctuates drastically, as it does in most of the country. Because the restaurant serves an average of 10 gallons of salsa every day and consistency in quality is paramount, it relies on canned tomatoes for the salsa, the most noted and oft-requested starter. You should select a good brand of canned crushed tomatoes that contain extra purée.

Makes approximately 3½ cups

1 28-ounce can crushed tomatoes
2 teaspoons minced white onion
3 minced jalapeños, preferably
   fresh
1 teaspoon ground *chile pequin,*
   chile de arbol, or cayenne

1 clove garlic, minced
½ teaspoon dried oregano
½ teaspoon salt

Canned tomatoes were developed in 1895 by the great French chef Escoffier. Tomato purée was readily available year-round, but he wanted to find a way to preserve crushed and chopped tomatoes for use through the winter. Escoffier worked with manufacturers in France's Rhone Valley to perfect the canned product, which became an immediate success. It caught on first in Italy and quickly found an audience in the United States. Rancho de Chimayó uses Angela Mia crushed tomatoes, a variety with meaty chunks and a rich purée, produced by Hunt's and usually available only to commercial kitchens.

Mix all the ingredients together. Chill the salsa for at least 30 minutes. Serve with tostada chips, tacos, or *flautas.*

   Tomato salsa keeps well for up to 5 days.

Pico de Gallo

Chunkier and hotter than tomato salsa, this cross between a relish and a salad is especially good in the late summer when fresh tomatoes and peppers are at their peak of flavor. The restaurant's *pico de gallo* is a family variation based on Mexican recipes.

Makes approximately 3 cups

1 medium tomato, chopped (about 1 cup)
¾ cup tomato juice
1 small bell pepper, chopped (about ¾ cup)
¼ cup chopped white onion
¼ cup chopped cilantro

4 to 5 chopped jalapeños, preferably fresh (about 1 tablespoon each)
1 clove garlic, minced
¼ teaspoon white pepper
¼ teaspoon salt

Combine all the ingredients in a medium bowl and mix well. Refrigerate for at least 30 minutes. Serve chilled with tostada chips or as an accompaniment to fajitas.

If kept refrigerated and tightly covered, *pico de gallo* can be made in advance. The crisp flavors won't fade before the end of the second day.

Tostadas

As Southwestern and Mexican food have increased in popularity, commercially-produced corn tortilla chips, traditionally known as tostadas, have appeared widely in the nation's grocery stores. Even the best of these chips, though, can't compete with the flavor and texture of warm, fresh tostadas. Rancho de Chimayó makes its chips as needed, at least twice a day. Most home cooks don't own deep fryers, so a heavy, high-sided skillet can be substituted. The Jaramillos recommend a wok, which although non-traditional, performs just as well and requires less oil.

Note: A deep-fry thermometer is needed for this dish.

Makes 48 or 72 chips, depending on size, enough for 4 to 6 people

12 5-inch corn tortillas
Cooking oil, preferably canola or
    corn, for deep frying

Salt or garlic salt to taste

At higher altitudes, the oil's temperature will need to be adjusted downward because deep-frying vaporizes the moisture in foods, and liquids vaporize at lower temperatures in higher altitudes. At 6,500 to 7,000 feet, the approximate altitude of Chimayó and nearby Santa Fe, the oil's temperature is best near 365°. At altitudes between 2,500 and 6,500 feet use a temperature in between. Experiment, and adjust the heat as needed.

Layer several thicknesses of paper towels on a counter near the stove.

Pour enough oil into a wok or heavy skillet to measure at least 1 inch in depth. Using the deep-fry thermometer as a guide, heat the oil to 375°. If the oil smokes before it reaches the proper temperature, it cannot be used for this recipe, because there is a danger of it catching fire. Make sure you are using fresh, high-quality oil.

While the oil is warming, cut each tortilla into 4 or 6 wedges. Four wedges work especially well if you plan to use the tostadas as the base for nachos.

When the thermometer reaches the frying temperature, test one chip. Drop the tortilla wedge into the oil. The chip should turn crisp before it darkens beyond a light golden color, a matter of seconds. Adjust the heat to raise or lower the oil temperature by a couple of degrees if necessary.

Gently drop 6 to 8 wedges into the oil. Stir constantly with a slotted spoon, using extreme caution to avoid splashing the hot oil and burning yourself. When the chips are crisp and light golden, remove them with the spoon and drain them on the paper towels. Check the thermometer again, adjusting the heat if necessary to maintain the correct temperature. Repeat the frying process with the remaining tortilla sections.

Salt, if desired, and serve warm with tomato salsa, guacamole, or *chile con queso*. Tostadas can be kept for up to 2 days in an airtight container. Rewarm the chips, uncovered, in a 250° oven before serving.

Burrell Tortilla

In the early years the Restaurante made this starter on special request for regular guest Mark Burrell. Its popularity with Mr. Burrell's dinner companions led the Jaramillos to decide to add the tasty but as yet nameless dish to the regular menu. The newly christened Burrell Tortilla quickly caught on with other diners, and it is now among the most requested appetizers. To make the dish at home, start with the freshest flour tortilla you can find. To get an authentic version, don't skimp on either the cheese or the chile sauce.

Makes 1 appetizer tortilla

1 7- to 8-inch flour tortilla
½ cup Green Chile Sauce (See recipe, page 64)

½ cup grated mild cheddar cheese

Preheat the oven to 350°.

Cut the tortilla into 4 wedges with a sharp knife or pizza cutter. Place the tortilla wedges back in a circle on a heatproof platter or baking sheet. Spoon the chile sauce evenly over the reassembled tortilla, and sprinkle the cheese over all.

Bake for 5 to 6 minutes, until the cheese is melted and a little bubbly. If the tortilla was cooked on a baking sheet, transfer the wedges to a decorative plate. Serve while piping hot with lots of napkins.

Guacamole

In Mexico guacamole dates back hundreds of years. It didn't become popular in northern New Mexico until regular shipments of California produce became available about midway through the twentieth century. The addition of Worcestershire sauce dates to the early 1960s when the condiment was a novel product in the Chimayó area.

Makes 2 to 2½ cups

4 medium Haas avocados, halved, seeded, and peeled
½ cup chopped, roasted green chile, preferably New Mexico green or Anaheim, fresh or frozen
½ medium tomato, chopped (about ½ cup)

2 teaspoons minced white onion
2 teaspoons mayonnaise
1 clove garlic, minced
½ teaspoon Worcestershire sauce
¼ teaspoon white pepper
¼ teaspoon salt

In a small bowl, mash the avocados with a potato masher or the back of a fork until reasonably smooth. Mix in the remaining ingredients. Spoon the guacamole into a serving bowl and accompany with tostada chips. Serve immediately.

Because guacamole darkens quickly, it is best mixed just before serving. The discoloration isn't harmful but it's unappealing in appearance. Adding lemon or lime juice to help keep the mixture green, as is often suggested in other books, alters the flavor. Placing the avocado seed back into the guacamole, another common notion, has little effect in prolonging its look. If you have to hold the guacamole for up to 30 or 45 minutes, place plastic wrap directly on its surface. The best way for cutting down on last-minute preparation time is to combine all the ingredients other than the avocados about an hour ahead of serving time. Just before eating, mash the avocados and fold in the remaining mixture.

Chile con Queso

Chile con queso *can be held in the double boiler over the lowest heat for an hour. It can also be refrigerated for 2 or 3 days and rewarmed in a double boiler. In either case, the addition of a tablespoon of milk may be needed to return the appetizer to its original consistency.* Chile con queso *makes a good party treat served in a chafing dish or on a warming tray.*

People who otherwise have relegated Velveeta cheese spread to fading childhood memories are usually surprised that the simple addition of chile and tomato can turn it into a wonderful dish. Velveeta is not a historical ingredient in northern New Mexican cooking, of course, but it does date back to the 1920s and was the first commercial cheese product available to Chimayó families. A welcome and versatile change from homemade goat cheese, it was widely embraced for its long shelf life, mild flavor, and superior texture in melting. While the wider availability of cheeses today has eliminated the use of Velveeta in most dishes, the cheese spread is still preferred by many Chimayó cooks for *chile con queso*. Rancho de Chimayó's recipe is based on one that won a local cooking contest the year the restaurant opened.

Makes 3 to 3½ cups

1 pound Velveeta cheese spread
½ cup chopped, roasted green
   chile, preferably New Mexico
   green or Anaheim, fresh or
   frozen

1 medium tomato, chopped (about
   1 cup)

Cut the Velveeta into 15 to 16 chunks, about 1 ounce each. Put the chunks in the top pan of a double boiler and place the pan over its water bath. Warm over medium-low heat.

Drain any accumulated liquid from the chile or tomatoes. When all of the Velveeta chunks have begun to melt, approximately 10 minutes, add the chile and tomatoes to the cheese spread. Continue to heat about 5 more minutes, until the Velveeta has melted into a smooth sauce, studded with bits of red and green. Pour into a bowl and serve warm with tostada chips, or use as a sauce for poached chicken breasts.

Nachos

Fresh jalapeños give these nachos a crisper, more refreshing bite than the pickled peppers that often top the snack elsewhere. Large, unbroken tostada chips are easiest to handle.

Serves 4 to 6

12 to 24 Tostada Chips, depending on size (See recipe, page 49)
¾ cup "Refried" Beans (See recipe, page 97)

¾ cup grated mild cheddar cheese
1 minced jalapeño, preferably fresh

Preheat the oven to 350°. If the "refried" beans have been refrigerated, warm them first in a small saucepan. With a butter knife, spread a thin layer of the beans across each chip. Place the tostadas on a heatproof serving platter or baking sheet. Top the chips with equal portions of the grated cheese and sprinkle jalapeños over all.

Bake for 5 to 7 minutes until the cheese is melted and a little bubbly. Watch carefully to avoid overcooking and toughening the cheese.

Serve the nachos immediately on the platter or transfer quickly from the baking sheet to a decorative plate. Tomato salsa is a good accompaniment, served on the side.

Nachos have become a top-selling snack throughout the United States, their popularity fueled by the "cheese sauce" variety served at sports stadiums and amusement parks. The burgeoning industry may have gone overboard when it asked New Mexico State University to develop a mild jalapeño, perfectly elliptical in shape, to ease slicing and insure that all patrons get the same size pieces.

ENSALADAS
Salads

Ensalada de Noche Buena
Christmas Eve Salad

Traditional to parts of Mexico, this salad is often a celebratory dish, historically served on Christmas Eve (*Noche Buena*). The salad became a part of the repertoire of New Mexico family dishes after supermarkets popped up in towns near Chimayó, making the ingredients easier to procure. Mayonnaise is a contemporary addition, a twist on the sour cream or creamy fresh cheese used more commonly in Mexico.

Serves 6

FOR THE DRESSING
1 medium lime
¼ cup mayonnaise
2 tablespoons honey
1 tablespoon cider vinegar
1 teaspoon dried ground red chile,
    preferably Chimayó, other New
    Mexico red, or *ancho*

1 clove garlic, minced
Salt to taste
2 tablespoons chopped cilantro
¼ cup peanuts, chopped
Seeds of 1 pomegranate
Lettuce leaves, optional, for garnish

For a more attractive, restaurant-style presentation of the oranges, start with the whole fruits. Peel each orange, removing the bitter white pith. Holding the first orange over the salad bowl and working with a sharp, flexible knife, slice into the orange along each side of its membranes, cutting to the orange's core. The sections will release. Squeeze any remaining juice from the membranes into the bowl. Discard the membranes and repeat with the remaining fruit. The process becomes easy with practice.

FOR THE SALAD

4 oranges, peeled and sectioned   2 medium bananas
¾ pound jícama, peeled

TO PREPARE THE DRESSING

Using a zester or paring knife, remove the green portion of the lime's peel in very thin strips. Cut the lime in half and squeeze the juice from both pieces. Put the lime zest and juice along with the remaining dressing ingredients into a blender container. Blend until well combined. Refrigerate until ready for use.

TO PREPARE THE SALAD

Cut the oranges and jícama into bite-size chunks. Mix them together in a bowl and refrigerate for at least an hour. Shortly before serving time, peel and slice the bananas. Add the bananas and the cilantro to the fruit and jícama mixture. Toss with the salad dressing. Turn out onto a serving platter, lined with lettuce leaves if desired. Top with peanuts and pomegranate seeds.

The salad dressing can be prepared a day ahead. For the salad, you can combine the jícama and oranges up to 8 hours in advance. Add the bananas and toss with the dressing just before serving time.

Fruit Salad

Chimayó is noted for its apples, but other fruits flourish in the town and surrounding valley too. Peach, apricot, cherry, and plum trees dot orchards throughout the area, their fruits ripening fragrantly with each summer's warm sun. The restaurant also uses other native New Mexican fruit, such as melons and raspberries, in its summer salads, occasionally adding tropical varieties more common to Mexico. This simple salad is at its best when it combines several fruits at their peak of flavor.

Serves 6

9 cups mixed fresh fruit (at least three kinds)

3 cups yogurt, cottage cheese, sherbet, or vanilla or fruit-flavored ice cream

Lettuce leaves, optional, for garnish

Cut any large fruit, such as honeydew melon or cantaloupe, into bite-size chunks. Halve smaller fruit, such as strawberries or cherries. Mix the fruit together in a large bowl and refrigerate for at least an hour.

Spoon about 1½ cups of the fruit mixture onto individual plates. Add ½ cup of yogurt, cottage cheese, ice cream, or sherbet to each plate of fruit. Garnish with lettuce leaves if desired.

Most fruits can be combined and refrigerated up to 6 hours ahead. Add raspberries, strawberries, or similarly fragile fruit within an hour of serving. If apples are among your chosen ingredients, don't cut them into chunks until just before serving time, to avoid possible discoloration. Apples may be pared, but leaving the red or green peel will add to the salad's bright hues.

Chef Salad

The Restaurante's festively attired staff contributes to its ambience. Women dress in peasant blouses with gaily colored skirts, while men wear black trousers and tuxedo shirts, accented by bright cummerbunds.

Serves 6

12 cups torn lettuce leaves
1½ pounds jalapeño jack cheese, cut into thin sticks
6 poached chicken breasts, shredded and combined with a tablespoon of pimiento and salt to taste
6 small tomatoes, cut into wedges

6 hard-boiled eggs, cut lengthwise into quarters
Carrot sticks, radishes, or other raw vegetables, for garnish
House Salad Dressing (See recipe, below) or other favorite salad dressing

Cover each dinner plate with 2 cups of the lettuce. Arrange equal portions of the cheese, chicken, tomatoes, and eggs over the lettuce. Garnish with the other vegetables on the side.

Serve accompanied with the salad dressing on the side.

House Salad Dressing

In 1991, cook Dave Bingham developed a special dressing for the restaurant inspired by three traditional products of the area, apple cider vinegar, honey, and red chile. The resulting sweet-sour dressing has just a hint of spice as well.

Makes approximately 1½ cups

¾ cup oil, preferably corn or canola
½ cup cider vinegar
3 tablespoons honey
1 tablespoon dried ground red chile, preferably Chimayó, other New Mexico red, or *ancho*

1 tablespoon minced fresh parsley
1 tablespoon minced white onion

Combine all the ingredients in a lidded jar, cover, and shake vigorously. Serve with mixed greens or the chef salad.

The dressing keeps for a week, covered and refrigerated.

Aguacates Rellenos
Avocados Stuffed with Shrimp or Chicken Salad

Makes 6 servings

6 cups boiled small or medium
    shrimp, peeled and chilled, or
6 poached chicken breasts, skinned,
    boned, shredded, and chilled
1 cup mayonnaise
½ cup chopped celery

½ cup diced pimiento
Salt and pepper to taste
6 avocados, preferably Haas
Lettuce leaves, for garnish
Carrot sticks or other fresh
    vegetables, optional

Mix the shrimp or chicken with the remaining ingredients in a medium-sized bowl. Season to taste with salt and pepper. Refrigerate for at least 30 minutes.

Slice the avocados in half, remove their pits, and peel them. On each dinner plate, arrange 2 avocado halves on lettuce leaves. Spoon equal portions of the chilled salad onto each plate, attractively mounding the salad over the avocados.

The shrimp or chicken salad can be prepared up to 8 hours ahead. Avocados should not be cut and peeled until serving time, to avoid discoloration.

The jovial figure of San Pasqual, the patron saint of the kitchen, graces many northern New Mexico homes. San Pasqual looks a little different depending upon each artist's interpretation, but the saint always appears to enjoy his food. His girth is cloaked in the brown robe of a Franciscan friar and an apron. Most paintings (retablos) and sculptures (bultos) show San Pasqual carrying a saucepan and a spoon as well.

CHILE SAUCES

Sauces based on dried red and fresh green chiles are the cornerstones of New Mexico cookery. Restaurant and home cooks take immense pride in their sauces, and they debate constantly the merits of their ingredients and cooking processes. Rancho de Chimayó's versions have been made the same way since the restaurant opened, although the heat of the particular batch of chile can vary the taste slightly from time to time. A blackboard in the kitchen announces which of the day's fresh pots of chile sauce are the hottest.

Red Chile Sauce

Makes approximately 6 cups

½ pound lean ground beef,
  preferably coarse ground
¾ cup dried ground red chile,
  preferably Chimayó, other New
  Mexico red, or *ancho*
1 tablespoon minced white onion
1 clove garlic, minced

½ teaspoon Worcestershire sauce
¾ teaspoon salt
¼ teaspoon white pepper
4 cups water
2 tablespoons cornstarch, dissolved
  in 2 tablespoons of water

Brown the ground beef over medium heat in a high-sided skillet until all of the pink color is gone. Add the chile, onion, garlic, Worcestershire sauce, salt, and white pepper and stir to combine. Pour the water slowly into the skillet while continuing to stir. Break up any lumps of chile. Continue heating the sauce and when it is warmed through, add the cornstarch.

Bring the mixture to a boil, and then reduce the heat to a simmer. Cook for about 10 minutes, stirring occasionally. The completed sauce should coat a spoon thickly and not taste of raw cornstarch. If it becomes too thick, add more water.

Serve the sauce warm with enchiladas, burritos, or other dishes.

Red chile sauce keeps in the refrigerator for 3 or 4 days. It freezes well. When reheating, add a little extra water if needed.

Genoveva Martinez, a cook at the restaurant since the day it opened, helped the Jaramillos develop this recipe. Mrs. Martinez remains a leading and lively influence in the kitchen today, even though she's well past the normal retirement age. Her eager smile brightens the kitchen almost every morning.

Vegetarian Red Chile Sauce

To remove red chile stains, soak the spot immediately in club soda. Launder in hot water.

Makes approximately 5 cups

¾ cup dried ground red chile, preferably Chimayó, other New Mexico red, or *ancho*
1 tablespoon minced white onion
1 clove garlic, minced
½ teaspoon salt
¼ teaspoon white pepper

4 cups vegetable broth, preferably, or water
2 tablespoons cornstarch, dissolved in 2 tablespoons water
Additional salt and white pepper to taste

Into a large, heavy saucepan, measure the chile, onion, garlic, salt, and pepper. Slowly add the broth or water, stirring carefully. Break up any lumps of chile. Cook the mixture over medium heat until warmed through, and add the cornstarch. Bring the sauce to a boil, then reduce the heat to a simmer. Cook for about 10 minutes, stirring occasionally. The completed sauce should coat a spoon thickly and no longer taste of raw cornstarch.

Serve the sauce warm with enchiladas, burritos, or other dishes.

Vegetarian red chile sauce keeps for up to 5 days in the refrigerator. It also freezes well.

Green Chile Sauce

If the heat of a chile sauce begins to set your mouth ablaze, don't drink water—it just inflames the heat. Reach for something sweet or creamy, like the honey that accompanies the Restaurante's sopaipillas, or a bite of cheese or sour cream.

Makes approximately 6 cups

½ pound lean ground beef, preferably coarse ground
4 cups water
2 cups chopped, roasted green chile, preferably New Mexico green or Anaheim, fresh or frozen
2 medium tomatoes, chopped, or 1 cup canned crushed tomatoes
2 teaspoons minced white onion

1 teaspoon salt
1 clove garlic, minced
¼ teaspoon white pepper
¼ teaspoon Worcestershire sauce
2 tablespoons cornstarch dissolved in 2 tablespoons water
Additional salt and white pepper to taste

Brown the ground beef over medium heat in a high-sided non-reactive skillet until all of the pink color is gone. While continuing to heat the skillet, pour in the water and add the chile, tomatoes, onion, salt, garlic, pepper, and Worcestershire sauce.

Bring the mixture to a boil, then lower the heat and simmer for 10 to 15 minutes. Add the cornstarch, and cook for 5 or 10 minutes more. The sauce should be thickened, but quite pourable, with no taste of raw cornstarch. Serve warm with burritos, enchiladas, or other dishes.

Green chile sauce keeps in the refrigerator for 3 to 4 days. It freezes well. When reheating, add a little extra water if needed.

Vegetarian Green Chile Sauce

Makes approximately 5 cups

4 cups vegetable broth, preferably, or water
2 cups chopped, roasted green chile, preferably New Mexico green or Anaheim, fresh or frozen
2 medium tomatoes, chopped, or 1 cup canned crushed tomatoes
2 teaspoons minced white onion

1 clove garlic, minced
½ teaspoon salt
¼ teaspoon white pepper
2 tablespoons cornstarch, dissolved in 2 tablespoons water
Additional salt and white pepper to taste

Combine all the ingredients except the cornstarch in a large saucepan and bring to a boil over medium-high heat. Reduce the mixture for 10 to 15 minutes. Add the cornstarch. Reduce the heat to a simmer, and cook for 5 to 10 minutes. The sauce should be thickened, but quite pourable, with no taste of raw cornstarch.

Vegetarian green chile sauce keeps up to 5 days in the refrigerator. It freezes well. When reheating, add a little extra water if needed.

The restaurant makes Green Chile Sauce 20 gallons at a time, combining equal proportions of mild and hot green chiles.

Sauce Picante for Shrimp

After long days at the restaurant, it's sometimes nice to have a change of pace from the regular menu. At home the Jaramillos mix up this fast and simple sauce to eat with cold boiled shrimp.

Makes approximately 1 cup

1 cup ketchup
2 teaspoons lemon juice
1 teaspoon Tabasco sauce

Salt and pepper to taste
Chopped cilantro, optional, for garnish

In a small bowl, mix together the ketchup, lemon juice, and Tabasco sauce. Adjust the seasoning with salt and pepper. Serve immediately, topped with cilantro if desired, as an accompaniment to cold boiled shrimp.

The sauce keeps for a week refrigerated.

As difficult as it was to procure some foodstuffs in the Chimayó area, shrimp have been available since colonial times. According to Fabiola Cabeza de Baca Gilbert, in her charming memoir The Good Life, *dried crustaceans were brought to the area by traders plying the Camino Real from central Mexico.*

Carne Adovada

Connoisseurs generally consider Chimayó's red chile to be the best available. Its flavorful balance of sweetness and heat is one of the secrets to Rancho de Chimayó's signature dish, *carne adovada*. Another variety of New Mexico red or even dried *ancho* chiles can be used in the recipe, but the resulting sauce won't be quite as complex. For the best results get dried Chimayó chiles locally or from one of the mail-order sources listed in the last chapter. *Carne adovada* is among the spiciest and most popular items on the restaurant's menu.

Serves 6 to 8

FOR THE CHILE SAUCE

8 ounces (about 25) whole dried
    red chile pods, preferably
    Chimayó, other New Mexico red,
    or *ancho*
4 cups water

1 tablespoon minced white onion
½ teaspoon Worcestershire sauce
½ teaspoon dried oregano
½ teaspoon salt
¼ teaspoon white pepper

A blender is required to achieve the proper sauce consistency for carne adovada. *A food processor does not yield the same result when puréeing the dried chiles.*

Carne adovada originated as a way to keep meat before the days of refrigeration. The fiery chile both flavored and preserved the fresh pork. The restaurant has no worries about keeping this dish today, especially when it's prepared by cook Kate Abeyta. Leftovers are never to be seen.

FOR THE MEAT
3 pounds boneless pork chops,
    trimmed of fat and cut into 1- to
    2-inch cubes.

FOR THE GARNISH
Lettuce and tomato, optional

TO PREPARE THE SAUCE
Preheat the oven to 300°.

Break the stems off the chile pods and discard the seeds. It isn't necessary to get rid of every seed, but most should be removed. Place the chiles in a sink or large bowl, rinse them carefully, and drain them.

Place the damp pods in one layer on a cookie sheet and roast them in the oven for about 5 minutes. Watch the pods carefully so as not to burn them. The chiles can have a little remaining moisture. Remove them from the oven and let them cool. Break each chile into 2 or 3 pieces.

In a blender, purée half the pods with 2 cups of the water. You will still be able to see tiny pieces of chile pulp, but they should be bound in a smooth, thick liquid. Pour the liquid into a large, heavy saucepan. Repeat with the remaining pods and water.

Add the remaining sauce ingredients to the chile purée and bring to a boil over medium-high heat. Simmer for 20 minutes, stirring occasionally. The mixture will thicken, but should remain a little soupy. Remove from heat.

TO PREPARE THE MEAT
While the chile sauce is simmering, oil a large, covered baking dish.

When the sauce has completed cooking, layer enough to cover fully the bottom of the baking dish. Top with the pork cubes. Pour the remaining sauce over the pork. There will be more sauce than meat.

Cover the dish and bake at 300° until the meat is meltingly tender and the sauce has cooked down, about 3½ hours. Check the meat, however, after 3 hours. The *carne adovada* can be left uncovered for the last few minutes of baking, if the sauce seems watery.

Serve garnished with lettuce and tomato on the side, if desired. Rancho de Chimayó accompanies the dish with *posole*.

The sauce can be made in advance and refrigerated for a day. The completed dish can be refrigerated for up to 3 days. Add a couple of tablespoons of water before reheating in the oven or on the stove.

Chicken Flautas

Originally from Mexico, *flautas* are little "flutes" of tortillas wrapped around chicken and deep-fried at a high temperature. Cooked properly, they are virtually greaseless. If you don't have a deep fat fryer, you can use a wok, as the Jaramillos suggest for preparations at home. It requires less oil than most skillets.

Note: A deep-fry thermometer is needed to monitor the oil's temperature.

Serves 5 to 6 as a main dish, 9 as an appetizer

FOR THE FILLING
1½ pounds boneless, skinless
   chicken breasts
Chicken broth or water to cover
   chicken breasts
2 tablespoons pimiento (1 2-ounce
   jar)

2 teaspoons chicken bouillon
   granules, optional
Salt to taste

FOR THE *FLAUTAS*
18 5-inch corn tortillas
Oil, preferably canola or corn, for
   deep-frying

FOR THE GARNISH
Guacamole and Tomato Salsa (See
   recipes, pages 51 and 47)

TO PREPARE THE FILLING
Poach the chicken breasts in the broth or water for about 15 minutes, or until they are cooked through. Drain them. When cool enough to handle, tear the meat into fine shreds. A food processor equipped with the plastic dough blade makes shredding chicken or any other meat easy work. Just pulse on and off a few times.

Combine the chicken, pimiento, and bouillon (optional) in a medium-sized bowl. Taste the mixture and add salt if needed. Set aside while you ready the tortillas.

TO PREPARE THE *FLAUTAS*
Layer several thicknesses of paper towels near the stove. Pour the oil into a heavy skillet or wok to a depth of at least 1 inch. Heat the oil until it ripples. With a pair of tongs, briefly dip each tortilla into the hot oil. In a matter of a few seconds the tortilla will become limp. Remove it immediately and

For pork flautas, use 1½ pounds of shredded pork loin. First bake the meat, covered in 3 to 4 cups of water to which half a white onion has been added, for about 1½ to 2 hours in a 350° oven. Cool and proceed as for chicken flautas, omitting the pimiento and the bouillon.

For vegetarian flautas, fill the tortillas with 3 cups of "refried" beans. If the beans have much liquid, heat them long enough to evaporate most of the moisture, or the flautas will become mushy.

Kids enjoy a contemporary Jaramillo creation based on the flauta. Start with a chorizo Americano, a.k.a. a hot dog. Slit the hot dog lengthwise and fill it with grated mild cheddar cheese. Wrap it tightly in a corn tortilla and deep-fry. Eat plain as a finger food, or top the dish with chile con queso.

drain it on the paper towels. If you don't act fast enough the tortilla will become crisp. Repeat the procedure with all the tortillas. Turn off the heat under the oil while filling the *flautas*.

Spoon 1½ to 2 tablespoons of filling on a tortilla and roll up tightly. Secure it with a toothpick. Set it aside and repeat with the remaining filling and tortillas.

Layer more paper towels if needed. Reheat the oil to 375° (or lower temperature at higher altitudes; see note on page 49), using the thermometer to monitor the temperature. If the oil smokes before reaching the proper temperature, it cannot be used for this recipe, because there is a danger of it catching fire. Make sure you are using high-quality oil.

When the oil has reached the correct temperature, add several of the *flautas*, using caution to avoid splashing the oil and burning yourself. Do not crowd the *flautas*. Cook them for about 2 minutes, turning occasionally, until golden-brown and crisp. Drain them on the paper towels. Repeat with the remaining *flautas*, adjusting the heat as needed to maintain the proper temperature.

Remove the toothpicks and serve immediately with guacamole and tomato salsa.

Pollo Al Estilo Chimayó
Chimayó Style Chicken

Makes 6 servings

FOR THE CHICKEN
6 skinless chicken breasts   Salt to taste

FOR THE TOPPING
3 cups Vegetarian Red Chile Sauce
   (See recipe, page 63), and ¾ to 1
   cup grated mild cheddar cheese
or
3 cups *chile con queso* (See recipe,
   page 52)

Poach the chicken breasts for 15 minutes, or until they are cooked through.
Salt to taste.

Arrange the chicken on serving plates. If topping with the vegetarian red
chile sauce, cover each breast with ½ cup of the sauce. Sprinkle the portions
with the cheese and run them under a broiler until the cheese is melted. To
top the chicken with *chile con queso*, just ladle the warm sauce over each
piece.

The Restaurante serves Pollo Al Estilo Chimayó accompanied with Spanish
rice and *calabacitas*.

Time-Life's esteemed cookbook series Foods of the World *covered the American West in a 1971 book, with Rancho de Chimayó among the handful of restaurants featured.* American Cooking: The Great West, *brought recognition, reviewers, and hungry patrons in increasing numbers. Pollo Al Estilo Chimayó was among the dishes included in the publication.*

Cheese Enchiladas

For a totally vegetarian dish, use the vegetarian red or green chile sauces and substitute soy cheese for the grated cheddar.

Chimayó enchiladas were traditionally stacked rather than rolled, contrary to the Mexican style seen most frequently in this country. You can make them with either green or red chile today, but in the past Chimayó cooks would have used red most of the year since they would have had access to fresh green pods only during the late summer and early fall. Restaurante cook Susie Trujillo specializes in preparing these zesty enchiladas today. Multiply this recipe by the number of people you plan to serve.

If you want to make cheese enchiladas at home for more than four guests, it may be simpler to take the non-traditional route and either roll the enchiladas or make a large casserole dish of the flat variety. If you want to roll them, fill each softened tortilla with an equal portion of the cheese and onion. Place them in a shallow baking dish, packed one beside the other. Top with the sauce and bake at 350° until the cheese is melted. If you make the enchiladas flat in a casserole dish, layer all the tortillas, cheese, onion, and sauce up to a depth of 3 inches and bake at 350° until heated through.

Makes 1 serving

3 5-inch corn tortillas
Oil, preferably canola or corn, to a
   depth of 1 inch
¾ cup Red or Green Chile Sauce
   (See recipes, pages 62 and 64)

1 teaspoon minced white onion
½ cup grated mild cheddar cheese

Arrange several layers of paper towels near the stove. Pour the oil into a skillet or sauté pan at least 6 inches in diameter. Heat the oil until it ripples.

With tongs, dip each tortilla into the hot oil. In a matter of seconds, the tortilla will become limp. Remove it immediately and drain it on the paper towels. If you don't act quickly enough, the tortilla will become crisp. Repeat the process with the rest of the tortillas.

Warm the chile sauce and set it nearby.

On a heatproof plate, layer the first tortilla with half of the onion and one-third of the chile sauce and cheese. Repeat for the second layer. Top with the third tortilla, then add the remaining chile sauce and sprinkle the cheese over all. Run the enchilada under a broiler until the cheese melts. Serve piping hot.

The Restaurante serves its enchilada plates with pinto beans.

Chicken Enchiladas with Blue Corn Tortillas and Green Chile

Cheese is the traditional enchilada filling, but meat has become a popular substitute in recent decades. In northern New Mexico the meat is almost always chicken. Rancho de Chimayó pairs it with another area product, blue corn tortillas. Upon their arrival several centuries ago, the Spanish settlers found the Pueblos cultivating blue corn. Along with its distinctive dark color, the blue corn flour possesses a more delicate texture, and a special nuttiness in flavor. The Jaramillos like the combination of the chicken enchiladas with their Green Chile Sauce, but the Red Chile Sauce can be used if you like. Multiply this recipe by the number of people you plan to serve. To make more than 4 servings of enchiladas, refer to the suggestions under Cheese Enchiladas (page 72).

Makes 1 serving

3 5-inch blue corn tortillas
Oil, preferably canola or corn, to a
  depth of 1 inch
¼ cup finely shredded poached
  chicken breast

1 teaspoon minced white onion
½ cup Green Chile Sauce (See
  recipe, page 64)
¼ cup grated mild cheddar cheese

Prepare the tortillas following the directions for the preceding recipe for Cheese Enchiladas (page 72).

Warm the chile sauce and the chicken. To layer the ingredients, top the first tortilla with half of the chicken and onion, and one-third of the chili sauce and cheese sauce. Repeat for the second layer. Top the stack with the third tortilla, then add the remaining chile sauce and sprinkle cheese over all. Run the enchilada under a broiler until the cheese melts. Serve piping hot.

For a side dish, the restaurant recommends pinto beans.

To make a "red enchilada," use just 2 to 3 tablespoons of Red Chile Sauce (page 62). A greater quantity can obliterate, rather than enhance, the chicken's flavor.

Only a few years ago, blue corn was scarcely known outside of New Mexico, but with the recent explosion of interest in Southwestern cooking, it is appearing nationwide in everything from popcorn to pancake batter. Blue corn tortillas make good tostadas and soft taco shells, but they are too fragile for flautas or hard-shell tacos. If you can't locate the tortillas locally, contact the mail-order sources listed in the last chapter or substitute regular corn tortillas.

TAMALES

New Mexico tamales historically consisted of a savory pork and chile filling coated with cornmeal dough, wrapped in softened corn husks, and steamed. A recipe for these tamales, and one for a newer vegetable-filled version, are included here.

Originally from Mexico, tamales came to New Mexico as a Christmas treat, perhaps because their labor-intensive preparation is simplified when you have enough people together for an assembly-line process. If possible, round up a few friends or family members to help. The work goes quickly with extra hands.

Whether you're making tamales alone or with assistance, clear off a table for your workspace and line up the bowls of corn husks, dough, and filling, and have a towel and scissors handy. You'll need a large plate or bowl for the wrapped tamales. Allow at least two hours for assembling the tamales if you are inexperienced. It will go faster with practice or additional help. The final steaming requires another hour or more.

Tamales can be plump or thin and shaped as long cylinders or as rounded pouches. Corn husks can be tied with strips of extra husk at both ends, or at the top of a pouch, or folded over at one end. Their appearance is limited only by your imagination. To assure that they cook fully, tamales should not be made any larger in weight than described in the recipes below. But they can be made smaller for appetizers.

Keep the dough loosely covered when working. The dough should be spread thin, on the smoother side of the corn husks, but not to the edges of the husks. Top with filling spread more thickly through the dough's center, stopping short of the dough's edges. Begin rolling the tamale into the desired shape, making sure that the dough's edges meet to enclose all of the filling. Secure the tamale by folding over an end of the husk or by tying with strips of additional husks.

Depending on the size of the corn husks, you may have to overlap two husks to form one tamale. Spread the dough over the husks together, just as if they were one.

To cook the tamales, a Dutch oven, a large saucepan, or a small stockpot works best. Use a metal vegetable steamer or improvise with a baking rack or metal colander over a couple of inches of water. If you own a Chinese bamboo steamer, it's workable too, used as you would regularly. Place the tamales into the steamer, packing loosely in criss-cross directions, or stand them on end. Allow enough space between them for the steam to rise effectively. Cover the pot and cook over simmering water. Two steamers may be necessary, or two batches required.

Pork Tamales

Makes 24 tamales of approximately 4 ounces each, about 12 main-dish servings

FOR THE FILLING

1½ pounds pork loin
1 medium white onion, chopped
2 cups water
2 tablespoons oil, preferably corn
    or canola
2 cloves garlic, minced
1 tablespoon flour

½ cup dried ground red chile,
    preferably Chimayó, other
    New Mexico red, or *ancho*
¾ teaspoon salt
¼ teaspoon cumin
⅛ teaspoon dried, ground oregano

FOR THE TAMALES

1 6-ounce package dried corn husks
6 cups *masa harina*
2 cups oil, preferably canola or
    corn

4½ cups water, or more as needed
2 teaspoons salt

TO PREPARE THE FILLING

Preheat the oven to 350°.

    Place the pork and the onion in a medium-sized baking dish and cover with the water. Bake for approximately 1½ hours, or until the meat is cooked through and pulls apart easily. Remove the pork from the broth. Set the meat aside to cool a few minutes, and refrigerate the broth. When the pork has cooled enough to handle, shred it finely, either with two forks, or with the dough blade in a food processor. Strain the broth after any fat has solidified on its surface. If the broth doesn't measure 2 cups, add water to make 2 cups of liquid. Reserve the pork and the broth.

    In a large heavy skillet, warm the oil over medium heat and add the minced garlic and the pork. Sprinkle the flour over the mixture and stir constantly for about a minute as the flour begins to brown. Add the ground chile, the reserved broth, and the salt, cumin, and oregano. Continue cooking over medium heat for about 30 minutes, or until the mixture has thickened and is almost dry. Watch carefully toward the end of the cooking time, stirring frequently so as not to burn. The filling will be meltingly tender. Reserve the mixture.

TO PREPARE THE CORN HUSKS

In a deep bowl or baking pan, soak the corn husks in hot water to cover. After 30 minutes the husks should be softened and pliable. Separate the husks and rinse them under warm running water to wash away any grit or brown silks. Soak them in more warm water until they are ready to use.

Two corn products are used regularly in northern New Mexican tamales: dried corn husks and masa harina, *a cornmeal mix also used in tortillas. Both are widely available throughout the Southwest and are appearing more frequently on the shelves of specialty food stores and well-stocked supermarkets nationally. If you can't find them locally, see the last chapter, New Mexico Products and Mail-Order Sources. There is no substitute for the* masa harina. *In place of the corn husks, it is possible to use lightweight aluminum foil, cut into 5- or 6-inch squares. A little of the corn flavor will be lost, but satisfactory tamales can be created. The tamales won't look as good in the foil, so remove it before serving.*

TO PREPARE THE *MASA*

Masa is the dough made from the *masa harina* cornmeal. Measure the *masa harina* into a large mixing bowl. Add the oil, water, and salt. Mix with a sturdy spoon, powerful electric mixer, or with your hands until smooth. When well-blended, the *masa* should have the consistency of a moist cookie dough. Add more water if needed for your preferred consistency.

ASSEMBLING THE TAMALES

Review the general tamale instructions preceding this tamale recipe. The amount of *masa* and filling used for each tamale should be approximately equal, but will vary depending on the size and shape of the tamale. To make 2 dozen 4-ounce tamales, use 2 tablespoons of *masa* and filling for each tamale.

Hold a corn husk flat on one hand. With a rubber spatula, spread a thin layer of *masa* across the husk and top with the filling. Roll the husk into the desired shape, using your imagination. Repeat the procedure until all the filling and *masa* are used.

COOKING THE TAMALES

Review the general tamale instructions for tips on steaming the tamales. Cook the tamales over simmering water for about 1 to 1¼ hours until the *masa* is firm and no longer sticks to the corn husk. Unwrap one tamale to check its consistency.

SERVING THE TAMALES

Tamales should be eaten warm. The corn husks are usually left on when tamales are served unadorned, to be removed by each guest before eating. These tamales are good topped with red chile sauce too, but the husks should be removed before adding the sauce.

Zucchini and Green Chile Tamales

Léona's de Chimayó makes savory vegetarian tamales for Rancho de Chimayó. Léona Tiede, for whom the company is named, is a neighbor of the Jaramillos. She developed the filling to combine distinctive New Mexico flavors in a delicious new way. The booming cottage industry has grown to employ not only Léona, her husband Dennis, and son Paul, but the entire Tiede family and other village residents. Their small factory, just down the road from the Restaurante, express-mails these and other kinds of tamales to anyone who would rather not make them at home. See the final chapter, New Mexico Mail-Order Products and Sources, for information about the tamales and other products of Léona's de Chimayó.

Makes 24 tamales of approximately 4 ounces each, about 12 main-dish servings

FOR THE FILLING

1 cup roasted, peeled green chile, undrained, preferably New Mexico green or Anaheim, fresh or frozen

¼ cup water
3 pounds fresh zucchini, grated
1 tablespoon salt, or more to taste
2 teaspoons minced garlic

FOR THE TAMALES

1 6-ounce package dried corn husks
6 cups *masa harina*
1⅔ cups oil, preferably canola or soybean

1 tablespoon salt
5½ cups water, or more as needed

TO PREPARE THE FILLING

In a small heavy saucepan, simmer the green chile and water over very low heat until the chile has darkened in color and most of the liquid has evaporated. Set aside briefly to cool.

Pour the green chile into a large bowl, add the zucchini, salt, and garlic, and mix well. Spoon the mixture into a colander or large strainer to drain any accumulated liquid. Reserve the filling.

TO PREPARE THE CORN HUSKS

In a deep bowl or baking pan, soak the corn husks in hot water to cover. After 30 minutes the husks should be softened and pliable. Separate the husks and rinse them under warm running water to wash away any grit or brown silks. Soak them in more warm water until they are ready to use.

If you don't plan to use the tamales in a day's time, freeze them prior to steaming. Take the tamales from the freezer and steam them unthawed, following the recipe's instructions. Steamed tamales keep for several days in the refrigerator, tightly covered, but also can be frozen without losing their quality. Reheat them by steaming for about 5 minutes, or until they are heated through.

Léona suggests other vegetable fillings such as mushrooms, spinach, Swiss chard, or onion. Yellow crookneck squash can be combined with an equal amount of zucchini, but it becomes a little too mushy alone. Cheddar cheese is a good filling too, especially when it is combined with green chile.

Léona's de Chimayó forms the tamales into long cylinders and then wraps them in parchment paper cut in 6-inch squares. While doing this is not essential for the home cook, it helps shape the tamales uniformly and looks attractive when a quantity of tamales are stacked together.

TO PREPARE THE *MASA*

Masa is the dough made from the *masa harina* cornmeal. Measure the *masa harina* into a large mixing bowl. Add the water, oil, and salt. Mix with a sturdy spoon, powerful electric mixer, or with your hands until smooth. When well blended, the *masa* should have the consistency of a moist cookie dough. Add more water if needed for your preferred consistency.

TO ASSEMBLE THE TAMALES

Review the general tamale instructions preceding the pork tamale recipe. The amount of *masa* and filling used for each tamale should be approximately equal, but will vary depending on the size and shape of the tamales. To make 2 dozen 4-ounce tamales, use 2 tablespoons each of *masa* and filling for each tamale.

Hold the corn husk flat on one hand. With a rubber spatula, spread a thin layer of *masa* across the husk and top with the filling. Roll the husk into the desired shape, using your imagination. Repeat the procedure until all the filling and *masa* are used.

TO STEAM THE TAMALES

Review the general tamale instructions for tips on steaming the tamales. Cook the tamales over simmering water for about 1 to 1¼ hours, or until the *masa* is firm and no longer sticks to the corn husk. Unwrap one tamale to check its consistency.

SERVING THE TAMALES

The tamales should be eaten warm. The corn husks are usually left on when tamales are served unadorned, to be removed by each guest before eating. The tamales are good topped with green chile sauce too, but the husks should be removed before adding the sauce.

Carne Asada

Famed New York food critic Mimi Sheraton is just one of the fans of the Restaurante's *carne asada*, a grilled tender New York strip steak smothered in green chile. The quality of the steak is paramount. Insist upon, and be willing to pay for, the best your local butcher offers.

Makes 1 serving

8 ounces New York strip steak
1 garlic clove, split in half
Salt to taste
½ cup Green Chile Sauce (See recipe, page 64)

2 tablespoons grated mild cheddar cheese

Preheat the grill or broiler.

Trim the steak of any exterior fat. Rub both sides of the steak with the garlic clove and then salt to taste. Let the meat come to room temperature before cooking it.

Grill or broil the steak to the preferred doneness, turning it once. Remove the meat and place it on a heatproof plate. Top it with the green chile sauce, and sprinkle the cheese over all. Place the plate under the broiler until the cheese melts. Serve immediately.

Real fans of fiery food may prefer the carne asada *without the cheese, which mellows the flavor.*

Bistec Solomillo
Ground Sirloin Steak

This simple preparation elevates ground beef well above the usual hamburger. As you would with *carne asada*, insist upon the best beef available. This hefty portion serves one at Rancho de Chimayó, but demure diners may prefer to split the dish in half.

Makes 1 or 2 servings

10 ounces lean ground sirloin
½ cup Red or Green Chile Sauce
  (See recipes, pages 62 and 64)

2 tablespoons grated mild cheddar
  cheese

Preheat the broiler.

Form the ground sirloin into one large or two smaller patties and broil to a preferred doneness. Broil close enough to the heat that the exterior of the meat chars slightly. Remove the beef and blot any accumulated grease with paper towels.

Arrange the ground sirloin on a heatproof plate or plates. Smother the meat with green or red chile sauce and sprinkle cheese over the top. Place the plate or plates under the broiler until the cheese melts. Serve hot.

Tacos

Tacos can be prepared similarly with all kinds of fillings. The Jaramillos also like chicken (prepared as for the chicken flautas), "refried" beans, and guacamole.

Makes 6 servings of 3 tacos each

FOR THE FILLING

2 pounds lean ground beef
¾ cup water
2 teaspoons minced white onion

½ teaspoon Worcestershire sauce
½ teaspoon salt
⅛ teaspoon pepper

FOR THE TACOS

18 taco shells
2 cups shredded lettuce, preferably romaine or iceberg
2 cups grated mild cheddar cheese

Tomato Salsa, as an accompaniment (See recipe, page 47)

TO PREPARE THE FILLING

In a large skillet, crumble the ground beef and add the water. Cook over medium heat until the meat loses all of its pink color. Pour the meat into a colander or large strainer to drain the water and accumulated fat.

Turn the meat into a large bowl and add the other ingredients. Mix well and set aside.

TO PREPARE THE TACOS

Preheat the oven to approximately 250°.

Arrange the taco shells on a baking sheet. Place the shells in the oven and lightly warm them, about 5 minutes.

For a buffet presentation, the filling, shells, lettuce, cheese, and salsa can be placed in separate bowls for your guests to help themselves. For a sit-down meal, fill each taco shell with 1½ to 2 tablespoons of the filling, topped by equal portions of the lettuce and cheese. Serve on a decorative platter with tomato salsa on the side.

Soft Tacos

Hard-shell tacos are better known, particularly outside the Southwest, but the soft version is almost as popular at Rancho de Chimayó.

Makes 6 servings of 3 tacos each

Oil, preferably corn or canola, to a
    depth of 1 inch
18 5-inch corn tortillas
1 recipe taco filling (See previous
    recipe)

1 cup grated mild cheddar cheese
Shredded lettuce, for garnish
Tomato Salsa, as an
    accompaniment (See recipe, page
    47)

Preheat the broiler.

Layer several thicknesses of paper towels near the stove. In a medium-sized skillet, heat the oil until it ripples. With tongs, dip a tortilla into the hot oil and cook it until it is softened and pliable, a matter of seconds. Drain the tortilla on the paper towels, blotting off all oil from the surface. Repeat with the remaining tortillas.

Spoon 1½ to 2 tablespoons of the taco filling near the center of each tortilla and carefully fold it in half. Place the filled tacos on a heatproof platter and top them with the grated cheese. Run the tacos under the broiler just until the cheese melts. Garnish with lettuce and serve with tomato salsa on the side.

Unlike their hard-shelled cousins, soft tacos should be eaten with a fork.

Burritos Al Estilo Madril

Warm flour tortillas can encircle an almost endless array of burrito fillings. Rancho de Chimayó's most requested burrito stars its spicy *carne adovada*, pork slow cooked in a rich red sauce of Chimayó chile. Cook Roberta Ortega makes a particularly tasty version of the burrito. The hearty dish was named by the Jaramillos in honor of another Chimayó resident, Jane Madril Martinez.

Makes 6 servings

6 7- to 8-inch flour tortillas
1 recipe *Carne Adovada* (See recipe, page 67)

¾ cup grated mild cheddar cheese
Lettuce, tomato, and radish, optional, for garnish

Preheat the oven to 300°.

Sprinkle a few drops of water over each tortilla. Stack the tortillas, and wrap them tightly in foil. Warm them in the oven for 15 to 20 minutes, until they are soft and pliable. Remove the tortillas from the oven and turn the heat up to broil.

To assemble the burritos, take one tortilla from the foil at a time and place it on a heatproof plate. Lightly drain the chile sauce from the *carne adovada* pork, and spoon about 1½ cups of the pork down the center of the tortilla. Roll up the tortilla snugly around the filling, arranging the seam down on the plate. Repeat with the remaining tortillas and pork.

Ladle the reserved sauce evenly over the burritos. The sauce should lightly cover the tortilla and pool around the burrito as well. Sprinkle 2 tablespoons of cheese over each burrito. Melt the cheese under the broiler just before serving.

Garnish with lettuce, tomato, and radish if desired. "Refried" beans or pinto beans are the favorite accompaniment to these burritos.

Flour tortillas first came to New Mexico from the nearby Mexican state of Sonora. Although wheat has never been a cash crop in Chimayó or the surrounding area, there was enough production to satisfy the basic demand for tortillas. Into the 1940s many Spanish villagers still threshed at least some of their own grain, using goats and other farm animals to separate the wheat from the chaff with their hooves.

Burritos de Refritos

Burritos can be stuffed with beef taco filling or chicken flauta filling, with leftover carne asada, sliced thin, or with a combination of meat and beans. Top with your choice of chile sauces.

Makes 6 servings

6 7- to 8-inch flour tortillas
"Refried" beans (See recipe, page 97)
Red or Green Chile Sauce (See recipes, pages 62 and 64, or, for a meatless burrito, Vegetarian Red or Green Chile Sauce, pages 63 and 65)

Grated mild cheddar cheese
Shredded lettuce, for garnish

Preheat the oven to 300°.

Sprinkle a few drops of water over each tortilla. Stack the tortillas, and wrap them tightly in foil. Warm them in the oven for 15 to 20 minutes, until they are soft and pliable. Remove the tortillas from the oven and turn the heat up to broil.

To assemble the burritos, take one tortilla from the foil at a time and place it on a heatproof plate. Spoon about 1½ cups of the "refried" beans down the center of the tortilla. Roll up the tortilla snugly around the filling, arranging the seam down on the plate. Repeat with the remaining tortillas and beans.

Top the burritos with a generous portion of the chile sauce and a sprinkling of cheese. Melt the cheese under the broiler. Garnish with the lettuce and serve. Spanish rice is the suggested accompaniment.

Sopaipillas Rellenas

Florence Jaramillo relates that this recipe evolved from a regular customer, Bernadita Ortega Vigil, who ordered a hamburger, but didn't want it on a bun. The restaurant served it to her instead in a *sopaipilla* with a topping of green chile and cheese. Over the years it developed into the current dish, which cook Joan Medina makes with particular skill.

Makes 6 servings

1½ cups beef taco filling or chicken *flauta* filling (See recipes, pages 81 and 69)

1½ cups cooked pinto beans (See recipe, page 95)

3 cups Green Chile Sauce (See recipe, page 64)

6 sopaipillas (½ recipe; See recipe, page 105)

¼ cup plus 2 tablespoons minced white onion

¾ cup grated mild cheddar cheese

Preheat the broiler. Warm the meat filling, beans, and chile sauce if they have been refrigerated.

Make the *sopaipillas* according to the recipe directions. While the *sopaipillas* are warm, gently slice open each with a serrated knife, creating an airy pouch. Spoon into each *sopaipilla* ¼ cup of your choice of meat fillings, and ¼ cup of the pinto beans. Arrange the *sopaipillas* on a heatproof platter or individual plates. Sprinkle a tablespoon of onion over the meat and beans. Top each *sopaipilla* with ½ cup green chile sauce and 2 tablespoons of cheese.

Place the stuffed *sopaipillas* under the broiler until the cheese is melted and bubbly. Serve immediately.

Huevos Rancheros

The Restaurante's version of huevos rancheros was one of the dishes selected by P.B.S. for inclusion in its "Great Chefs of the West" series, filmed in the early 1980s. The television segment featured cook Manuel Aragon, who takes particular pride in his preparation of the dish.

Although usually associated with breakfast, huevos rancheros is a hearty regional favorite at any time of the day, almost always accompanied by "refried" beans. The Jaramillos like it with Spanish rice as well.

Makes 6 servings

Oil, preferably corn or canola, to a
   depth of ½ inch
6 5-inch corn tortillas
12 eggs

2 to 3 cups Green Chile Sauce,
   warmed (See recipe, page 64)
Shredded lettuce and chopped
   tomato, for garnish

Arrange several layers of paper towels near the stove.

Heat the oil in a large skillet until it ripples. With tongs, dip a tortilla into the hot oil and cook it until it is softened and pliable, a matter of seconds. Remove the tortilla immediately and drain it on the paper towels. If you don't act quickly enough, the tortilla will become crisp. Repeat with the rest of the tortillas. Carefully pour out of the skillet all but enough oil to generously coat its surface. Reserve the extra oil.

Arrange each tortilla on a plate and set aside.

Place the skillet back on the stove and heat the oil over low heat. Fry the eggs, 2 to 3 at a time, turning once after the whites have set and the yolk has thickened. (For health reasons, each should be fried until the yolk sets.) Top each tortilla with two eggs, arranged side by side. Continue until all the eggs are fried, adding a bit of the reserved oil when the skillet becomes dry.

Pour ⅓ to ½ cup of green chile sauce over each serving. Garnish the plates with lettuce and tomato. Serve with scoops of "refried" beans and Spanish rice, if desired.

Torta de Huevo con Chile y Carne
Omelette with Chile and Meat

Chiles rellenos are one of New Mexico's best-known dishes, but the flavorful chiles raised in Chimayó are usually too small to stuff in the typical preparation. These mounded omelettes developed as a way of incorporating the same flavors. Be sure to read through the preparation instructions before beginning to cook the *tortas*.

If you're not a regular omelette maker or an experienced fry cook, the technique for shaping these tortas *can be a little tricky. Practice on one or two servings for yourself before planning to present this to guests. If you aren't happy with the appearance of your results after a few tries, this combination of ingredients yields tasty scrambled eggs.*

Makes 6 servings of 2 tortas *each*

FOR THE MEAT MIXTURE

1 pound lean ground beef
¼ cup chopped white onion
1 clove garlic, minced

1 teaspoon Worcestershire sauce
Salt to taste

FOR THE *TORTAS*

1¾ pounds chopped roasted and
   peeled green chile, preferably
   New Mexico green or Anaheim,
   fresh or frozen

2 cups grated mild cheddar cheese
12 eggs
1½ cups milk
Oil

TO PREPARE THE MEAT MIXTURE

In a medium skillet, sauté the ground beef with the onion and garlic until it is cooked through. Add the Worcestershire sauce and salt to taste. Set the meat aside to cool, and reserve for later use.

TO PREPARE THE *TORTAS*

Lightly drain the green chile and spread half on a baking sheet in a solid, shallow layer, square or rectangular in shape. Spread half of the reserved ground beef mixture evenly over the chile and then top it with half of the cheese. Layer the remaining chile, ground beef, and cheese over the first set of layers. With a spatula, cut the layers into 12 equal portions. Use the spatula to separate each portion from the others, creating 12 distinct little parcels. Set aside the baking sheet.

In a mixing bowl, beat the eggs and the milk lightly with a whisk or fork until they are combined well.

Oil and heat a griddle or skillet. The number of *tortas* made at a time depends on the size of the cooking surface and the cook's confidence in watching and turning the *tortas*. A griddle that fits over two burners is large enough for cooking all the *tortas* at once, ideal if the cook has had a little practice.

If you don't have a griddle, the *tortas* can be made in smaller numbers in a skillet. Heat the oven to 250° so that each batch of *tortas* can be kept warm while the rest are completed. A 9-inch skillet works well for preparing 2 at a time. A 12-inch pan can accommodate 3 or 4 at once. Be sure the skillet is especially well-oiled or you will have difficulty in making successive batches of the *tortas*.

Pour the eggs onto the hot griddle or skillet. Quickly slide a spatula under each parcel of the filling and gently place on the layer of cooking eggs, spacing the filling "packages" equally on the griddle or skillet, at least a couple of inches from each other and from the pan's edges. As the eggs set, use the spatula to cut them into 12 rectangles slightly larger than the filling, which should now be in the center of each rectangle.

When the eggs have almost cooked through, a matter of a minute or two more, slide the spatula under the egg mixture extending beyond each filling. Working quickly but carefully, flip the cooked eggs up around the filling, creating compact mounded *tortas*. Turn each one over to finish cooking, another minute or two. The *tortas* will be lightly browned. If you are making the *tortas* in batches, slip the finished batches into the warm oven while completing the rest.

Serve the *tortas* hot, 2 per plate. Spanish rice, beans, or a crisp green salad are good accompaniments.

FAJITAS

In the mid-1980s, as Southwestern food spread in popularity faster than a range fire, patrons besieged Rancho de Chimayó with requests for fajitas. A Texas concoction, "fajitas" literally translates from Spanish as "sashes" or "strips." Tender strips of marinated meat are wrapped in warm tortillas and topped with savory vegetables and dollops of a spicy relish. While New Mexicans distrust many Texas imports, this one has won a fair measure of acceptance.

Beef Fajitas

Makes 6 to 8 servings

FOR THE BEEF FILLING

4 pounds flank steak
1 cup good-quality cold-pressed olive oil
2 tablespoons ground *chile pequin*, *chile de arbol*, or cayenne
2 cloves garlic

1 tablespoon lime juice
1 teaspoon white pepper
1 teaspoon salt
Generous dash A-1 Steak Sauce
3 tablespoons clarified butter, or more as needed

FOR THE VEGETABLE TOPPING

1 bell pepper, sliced in vertical strips
1 to 2 large onions, sliced in strips
2 medium tomatoes, cut into wedges

1 dozen medium mushrooms, sliced thin

Flour tortillas, 2 to 3 per person
Pico de Gallo and Guacamole, as accompaniments (See recipes, pages 48 and 51)

TO PREPARE THE BEEF FILLING

Slice the steak against the grain into thin strips and place the strips in a large bowl or pan. Combine the rest of the filling ingredients, except for the butter, and pour them over the steak, tossing to coat. Marinate the beef, refrigerated, for at least 5 hours or overnight.

Pour the marinade and steak into a large skillet and cook over medium-low heat until the strips are cooked through and tender. Drain the liquid from the pan. Add the 3 tablespoons of butter, and heat quickly just until the butter coats the strips and the meat crisps slightly. Turn the meat out on one side of a large serving platter and return the skillet to the stove.

TO PREPARE THE VEGETABLE TOPPING

Add the vegetables to the skillet, and sauté them briefly over medium heat until they are crisp-tender. If the mixture is too dry, add a little extra butter, scraping up any browned bits from the pan's surface. Arrange the mixture beside the beef on the serving platter.

TO ASSEMBLE THE FAJITAS

Present the meat and vegetables at the table with warm tortillas, *pico de gallo*, and guacamole. Each guest cups the tortilla and fills it with portions of beef and vegetables, adding spoonfuls of *pico de gallo* and guacamole according to taste. Tortillas of about 6 inches are a little easier to handle than the larger size, if you have a choice.

Serve the fajitas with beans if you like, but they can be a meal in themselves.

Chicken Fajitas

Makes 6 to 8 servings

FOR THE CHICKEN FILLING

4 pounds boneless, skinless chicken
   breasts
1 cup good-quality cold-pressed
   olive oil
2 tablespoons ground *chile pequin*,
   chile de arbol, or cayenne
1 teaspoon white pepper

1 clove garlic
¾ teaspoon salt
Generous dash A-1 Steak Sauce
4 tablespoons clarified butter, or
   more as needed
2 teaspoons flour

FOR THE VEGETABLE TOPPING

1 bell pepper, sliced in vertical
   strips
1 to 2 large onions, sliced in strips
2 medium tomatoes, cut into
   wedges

1 dozen medium mushrooms,
   sliced thin

Flour tortillas, 2 to 3 per person
Pico de Gallo and Guacamole, as
   accompaniments (See recipes,
   pages 48 and 51)

TO PREPARE THE CHICKEN FILLING

Lightly pound the chicken breasts. Cut them into thin strips, and place the strips in a large bowl or pan. Combine the rest of the ingredients, except for the butter and flour, and pour them over the chicken, tossing to coat. Marinate the chicken, refrigerated, for at least 4 hours or overnight.

Lightly drain the marinade from the chicken and discard the marinade. Add the 4 tablespoons of butter to a large skillet, and heat. Spoon the chicken strips into the skillet and dust with the flour. Sauté at medium-high heat until the strips are cooked through and tender. Turn the chicken out onto one side of a large serving platter and return the skillet to the stove.

TO PREPARE THE VEGETABLE TOPPING

Add the vegetables to the skillet, returning the heat to medium-high. Sauté briefly until the vegetables are crisp-tender. If the mixture is too dry, add a little extra butter, scraping up any browned bits from the pan's surface. Arrange the vegetables beside the chicken on the serving platter.

For vegetarian fajitas, increase the amounts of the vegetables used as the fajita topping, or add zucchini or yellow squash. Marinate the vegetables in olive oil, lime juice, garlic, white pepper, and salt to taste. Sauté the mixture in butter or more olive oil as you would for the fajita topping.

TO ASSEMBLE THE FAJITAS

Present the chicken and vegetables at the table with warm tortillas, *pico de gallo*, and guacamole. Each guest cups the tortilla and fills it with portions of chicken and vegetables, adding spoonfuls of *pico de gallo* and guacamole according to taste. Tortillas of about 6 inches are a little easier to handle than the larger size, if you have a choice.

Cabrito
Roasted Young Goat

For festive spring and summer family gatherings, *cabrito* is the meat of choice, roasted in a pit, on a spit, or in the oven. The young goat's meat is a little stronger in flavor than baby lamb. When it is cooked correctly, it can be quite tender. The Jaramillos like the style of preparation used by their neighbor Nolia Martinez, suggested here. If you take on the challenge of Mrs. Martinez's recipe, plan to bake the goat all day or overnight.

Note: A large roasting pan, something beyond the usual Thanksgiving turkey size, is needed for the *cabrito*. If you have no such pan, a suitable version can be created with a large, heavy baking sheet and a roll of heavyweight aluminum foil. Using foil at least 2 or 3 layers thick, fashion a pouch large enough to hold the goat sections. Crimp together the edges of the foil well, so that none of the cooking liquid will be able to leak out. Place the pouch on the baking sheet to support the bulk of the goat's weight.

Makes about 35 servings

FOR THE *CABRITO*

1 kid, about 30 pounds, quartered
1 medium head of garlic, peeled
⅓ cup dried, ground ginger

3 cups water
Salt and pepper to taste

FOR THE BARBECUE SAUCE

2 tablespoons oil, preferably corn
   or canola
1 cup chopped white onion
1 cup chopped celery

1 cup water
½ cup ketchup
⅓ cup cider vinegar
½ teaspoon ground nutmeg

FOR THE GRAVY

4 tablespoons cornstarch dissolved
   in 4 tablespoons water
1 clove garlic, minced

½ teaspoon dried, ground ginger
Salt and pepper to taste

TO PREPARE THE *CABRITO*

Preheat the oven to 400°.

Rinse the kid and dry it with paper towels. Halve the individual garlic cloves. Cut small slits on the goat legs and other surfaces and insert the garlic halves into the slits. Rub the entire surface of the meat with the ginger and sprinkle it with salt and pepper.

Arrange the kid in a large roasting pan. Roast it uncovered for 30 minutes,

At this time, goat meat is not federally-inspected, so it is not found in supermarkets. Particularly in Hispanic, Latino, and Greek communities, butchers often know of reliable sources for cleaned and dressed young goats. If you find a single goat leg or hindquarter, usually about 5 pounds, it will serve 6 generously and can be prepared by the same method, only with much less challenge. Reduce the roasting time at 400° by 10 minutes, and the cooking at 350° by 20 minutes. Bake at 325° for approximately 3½ hours.

While California is the state most celebrated for its garlic farming, white-skinned garlic grows well in the Dixon-Velarde area near Chimayó and is sold in northern New Mexico markets and roadside stands. Like chiles, garlic is often strung or braided into attractive ristras.

browning the surface. Remove the pan from the oven and lower the heat to 350°. Pour the water over the meat, and cover the pan tightly with foil. Return the kid to the oven and bake for 1 hour. Reduce the heat to 325° and continue to bake until the meat is well-cooked and quite tender, separating easily from the bone. The total cooking time will be 25 to 30 minutes a pound, about 11 hours of baking at 325°. Make the barbecue sauce below, get a good night's sleep, or otherwise occupy yourself while the *cabrito* cooks.

Remove the *cabrito* from the oven, and drain the accumulated cooking liquid, usually about 6 cups, into a saucepan to make the gravy. Let the *cabrito* sit for 15 to 30 minutes before pulling the meat from the bones. Allow plenty of time to ready the meat for serving.

TO PREPARE THE BARBECUE SAUCE

While the *cabrito* bakes, prepare the barbecue sauce. In a medium skillet, heat the oil and add the onion and celery. Brown the vegetables, stirring occasionally. Mix in the remaining ingredients and simmer for 25 to 30 minutes until the mixture is thickened. Refrigerate the sauce until the *cabrito* is cooked. Serve the sauce warm or chilled.

TO PREPARE THE GRAVY

To the saucepan with the meat drippings, add the cornstarch, garlic, and ginger, and bring to a boil. Reduce the heat and simmer 5 minutes. Season with salt and pepper. Reserve over very low heat.

TO SERVE THE *CABRITO*

Serve the cabrito warm, on large platters accompanied by bowls of gravy and barbecue sauce. Mix some of the meat with the barbecue sauce, if desired.

COMIDAS ADICIONALES
Side Dishes

Pinto Beans

The humble but nutrient-rich pinto bean derives its name from its reddish-brown color and cream-colored spots. A pot of these beans regularly simmers on a back burner in most Chimayó homes. At the restaurant, the bean pot cooks 50 gallons of the popular staple at a time.

The main secret to good beans is long cooking at low heat. When they are ready to serve, beans should hold their shape, but be smooth in texture. Don't cook them so fast or for so long that they become mushy. Cooked beans lose their spots, becoming pinkish-brown in color. The recipe's small quantity of oil adds a slightly rich unctuousness without making the beans greasy. While the cooking time is lengthy, the recipe is simple and almost foolproof.

If there isn't time to soak the beans at least 4 hours, you can use a shortcut. Place the beans in a pot and add about twice as much water. Bring to a boil, and boil the beans for 4 or 5 minutes. Remove the pot from the heat, cover, and let it stand for about 1 hour. Discard the soaking water, rinse the beans, and proceed according to the recipe.

As a variation, you can add 1 or 2 minced cloves of garlic to the beans at the time the oil and salt are added. The beans also can be topped with red or green chile sauce at the conclusion of their cooking. Add grated mild cheddar cheese if desired.

Epazote, a pungent wild herb often available in Hispanic and Latino markets, and through mail-order sources (see the last chapter), may be added to the beans toward the end of their cooking time. Epazote helps relieve gas. It may be used fresh, but it is commonly sold dried.

Whoever said that patience is a virtue may have been trying to rationalize the process of cooking beans at a lofty altitude. The cooking time lengthens the higher you ascend, requiring more water as well. At around 6,500 to 7,000 feet, as in Chimayó or Santa Fe, start the recipe using 10 cups of water rather than 8, and plan for 3½ to 5 hours of cooking time. You will likely need to add more hot water later in the simmering process. Add the oil and salt after about 3 hours of cooking.

Serves 6

1½ cups pinto beans
8 cups water, or more as needed
1 teaspoon oil, preferably corn or canola

1 teaspoon salt, plus additional to taste

Pick through the beans and rinse them carefully, looking for any gravel or grit. Soak the beans for at least 4 hours, or, preferably, overnight.

Drain the beans and add them to a stockpot or a large, heavy saucepan. Cover them with the 8 cups of water. Simmer the beans, uncovered, over low heat. Plan on a total cooking time of around 2 to 2½ hours. The hardness of the water, the altitude, and the particular beans' obstinacy can all affect the timing.

After 1 hour, stir the beans up from the bottom and check the water level. If there is not at least an inch more water than beans, add enough hot water to bring it to that level. Check the beans after another 30 minutes, repeating the process. Add the oil and salt after the beans are well-softened, and continue simmering. Check every 15 minutes, keeping the level of the water just above the beans. The beans are done when they are soft and creamy but not mushy, with each bean retaining its shape. There should be extra liquid at the completion of the cooking time, although the beans should not be soupy.

Serve immediately or cover and keep warm for 1 hour.

Pinto beans can be cooked a day before serving. Leftovers will keep another 3 or 4 days, if well-drained and tightly covered. Discard the beans if they begin to sour. This recipe freezes well.

"Refried" Beans

Any "refried" bean dish on the Rancho de Chimayó menu really has no more fat than the regular pinto beans. Because of contemporary health considerations, the restaurant now simply serves a warm bean purée as a substitute for the traditional mashed beans fried in lard.

To prepare the dish Chimayó style, start with pinto beans cooked according to the previous recipe. Using a potato masher or food processor, mash or process the desired quantity of beans with a little liquid until smooth and moist. Rewarm the beans and serve.

If you would like to stay truer to tradition, heat a few tablespoons of lard or bacon fat. For an alternative, a cold-pressed peanut oil adds a contemporary flavor without cholesterol. Add to the fat or oil a touch of minced garlic if desired, and add a quantity of pinto beans with their cooking liquid. Mash the beans with a potato masher as they fry. Heat the beans until they thicken and most of the liquid evaporates. Serve immediately.

Travel connoisseur Andrew Harper, in a 1990 edition of his Hideaways Report, *praised the Restaurante's lunches and dinners as "exquisite," and the "value-priced" lodging at the accompanying Hacienda "delightful."*

Posole

A couple of dried red chile pods, and/or a teaspoon or two of oregano or minced garlic, are tasty additions to posole. About ½ pound cubed pork can be added to create a heartier stew for a main dish. Cook the posole as described.

Canned hominy is often suggested as a substitute for posole. It makes a tolerable stand-in, but it has none of the subtle corn flavor or the rougher texture of true posole. If you can't locate either dried or frozen posole in a supermarket or specialty store, consider ordering it from one of the mail-order sources in the final chapter.

Along with beans, *posole* became a staple in the early Spanish settlers' subsistence diet, adopted from the Pueblo Indians. The summer's corn crop was removed from the cob, treated with lime (the mineral, not the fruit), and dried. The large white or yellow kernels have a subtle but delicious taste that one young restaurant guest likened to "underwater popcorn." Rancho de Chimayó prefers a very white *posole* to contrast with the vibrant colors of most of its main dishes. Traditionally the corn was stewed with pork, but today the restaurant serves it as a starchy side dish, without meat. On occasions like *Las Posadas* and Christmas, *posole* takes a centerpiece role, often dressed up with red chile pods and other spices, and made with pork.

Serves 6

1 cup dried or 1½ cups frozen
  posole
8 cups water, or more as needed

1 teaspoon salt, plus additional to
  taste

Dried *posole* should be soaked at least 4 hours or overnight. Rinse either kind of *posole* to eliminate the lime taste from the corn, and drain. (For a shortcut method of soaking, follow the instructions suggested with the Pinto Beans, page 95.)

Place the *posole* in a large heavy saucepan or stockpot and cover with the 8 cups of water. Add the salt. Bring the *posole* to a boil. Reduce the heat to medium-low and simmer uncovered. The total cooking time will be 1¼ to 2 hours, but it is variable.

After 1 hour, stir the *posole* up from the bottom and check the water level. If there is not an inch more water than *posole*, add enough hot water to bring it to that level. Simmer the *posole* until it is puffed and tender, checking at 15-minute intervals and adding additional water if necessary. At the end of the cooking time most of the water should be absorbed. Keep the *posole* warm for up to an hour, or serve immediately.

If you are cooking at high altitude, start the *posole* with 2 additional cups of water and plan on a total cooking time of 1¾ to 2½ hours.

Spanish Rice

For a totally vegetarian version of Spanish rice, exclude the Worcestershire sauce, which has anchovies among its many ingredients.

Because the rice and sauce are cooked separately in this recipe, the vegetables don't end up overcooked or mushy.

Serves 6

FOR THE RICE

1 cup rice
Water

Salt to taste

FOR THE SAUCE

1 14½-ounce can whole tomatoes, drained and chopped (juice reserved)
1 8-ounce can tomato sauce
½ cup chopped celery
¼ cup chopped bell pepper

¼ cup chopped white onion
1 clove garlic, minced
¼ teaspoon black pepper
¼ teaspoon paprika
¼ teaspoon Worcestershire sauce
Salt to taste

TO PREPARE THE RICE

Cook the rice according to the package directions or your favorite method, omitting any butter. Turn off the heat and let the rice stand covered for five minutes.

TO PREPARE THE SAUCE

While the rice is cooking, begin the sauce preparations. Add all of the sauce ingredients to a large pan and bring to a boil over medium heat. Reduce the heat and simmer, stirring occasionally, until the vegetables are tender, about 15 minutes. Add a little of the reserved tomato liquid if the mixture begins to dry out. The sauce should be thick but remain moist.

ASSEMBLING THE DISH

Pour the rice into the sauce and mix thoroughly. Serve immediately.

You can make the sauce in advance, undercooking it by a couple of minutes and refrigerating it for up to 24 hours. Prepare the rice just before serving, reheating the sauce while the rice is cooking.

Roasted Green Chile

For eating alone as a side dish, most people will want a somewhat mild chile, such as the Big Jim variety of New Mexico green. The Big Jim is one of New Mexico's best-known chiles. It is named for Jim Lytle, who with scientist Roy Nakayama developed the variety. The hefty pods grow best in southern New Mexico's Mesilla Valley, where the Lytles have their farm. The Jaramillos get much of their New Mexico green from the Lytle family, ordering it by the pick-up truck load. You can get this tasty chile directly from the Lytles as well, through their mail-order business and retail store, the Hatch Chile Express. Other mail-order sources sell it as well.

One sure sign of autumn approaching in New Mexico is the distinctive smell of roasting green chile. At this time, when the local harvest is at its peak, the Jaramillos serve the roasted chile as a side dish. The roasting process blisters the inedible skin, allowing it to be easily removed, and mellows the pods' pungent flavor.

Throughout Chimayó and the rest of New Mexico, families and neighbors roast chiles by the bushel or 40-pound sack. Fresh-picked chiles fill large wire cages that rotate on a spit over an open fire. Some of the chiles are devoured while still warm, and much of the crop is frozen for the rest of the year. It isn't necessary, though, to have a wire cage to prepare enough roasted chile for a home meal. You can recreate the process in your kitchen.

Makes 6 servings

12 medium to large fresh New Mexico green or Anaheim chiles

Salt to taste

Wash the chiles and pat them dry. Follow one of the methods for roasting and peeling fresh chiles described under "Chiles" in the final chapter, New Mexico Products and Mail-Order Sources.

Remove the stems and most of the seeds from the roasted, peeled pods. Chop the chiles into bite-size pieces, salt to taste, and serve warm.

Calabacitas

For spicier calabacitas, *increase the amount of green chile to about 1 cup, or more or less to taste. For a totally vegetarian version, leave out the cheese or substitute soy cheese instead.*

The Spanish settlers of Chimayó, following the example of the Pueblos, grew a good deal of squash, one of the few vegetables that flourished in the area. During the harvest season they feasted on this mélange of zucchini and yellow crookneck squash mixed with green chile and corn, drying the remainder of the summer squash crop for use during the winter months. The restaurant can now offer fresh *calabacitas* year-round, but the Jaramillos take particular pride in the dish when the local vegetables are at their peak. *Calabacitas* can double as a light meatless main dish.

Makes 6 to 8 side-dish or 4 main-dish servings

4 tablespoons oil, preferably corn or canola

4 to 6 medium zucchini, or a mix of zucchini and other summer squash, to yield approximately 5 cups when sliced into bite-size chunks

1 medium white onion, chopped

2 cups corn, fresh or frozen

½ cup chopped, roasted green chile, preferably New Mexico green or Anaheim, fresh or frozen

3 tablespoons water, or more as needed

½ teaspoon salt

Grated mild cheddar cheese, optional, for garnish

In a large skillet, heat the oil and add the squash and the onion. Sauté the vegetables over medium heat until they begin to wilt. Add the corn, green chile, water, and salt. Cook, covered, over low heat until tender, about 15 to 20 minutes. Another tablespoon or two of water can be added if the vegetables become dry. Remove from the heat and mix in the cheese, if desired. Serve immediately.

Torta de Huevo Tradicional
Egg Patties

At 6,500 to 7,000 feet, the altitude of Chimayó and Santa Fe, the batter will rise more easily, so less leavening is needed. Use just a pinch of baking powder and fry between 360° and 365°. At altitudes between 2,500 and 6,500 feet, adjust the baking powder and temperature accordingly.

Don't let the simplicity of this dish cause you to pass it by. Although not regularly on the restaurant menu, these light, crispy egg fritters are a Jaramillo family favorite, especially when prepared by Genoveva Martinez, the Restaurante's senior cook. Steeped in tradition, the *tortas* are common in northern New Mexico households during Lent, when meat is avoided. The *tortas* also appear on Easter menus because of the association of eggs with new life. Try them as a light main course too.

Makes 6 side-dish or 2 to 3 main-dish servings

3 eggs
3 tablespoons flour
Scant ¼ teaspoon baking powder
Pinch salt
Oil, preferably corn or canola, to a
    depth of 1 inch

Vegetarian Red Chile Sauce or
    Vegetarian Green Chile Sauce for
    topping (See recipes, pages 63
    and 65)

Separate the eggs, dropping the whites into a medium-sized non-plastic mixing bowl and placing the yolks in a small bowl. Whip the yolks lightly with a fork or whisk. Stir in the flour, baking powder, and salt, and set aside.

Beat the egg whites with a whisk or mixer at high speed until they are stiff. Gently fold the egg yolk mixture into the egg whites.

Layer several thicknesses of paper towels near the stove. In a heavy skillet, heat the oil to between 370° and 375°. Drop a large spoonful of the batter gently into the oil. Within seconds the *torta* should puff up by 50 percent or more. Turn the patty at least once while cooking. Fry it until it is deep golden-brown and crisp.

Remove the first *torta* with a slotted spoon and drain it on the paper towels. Cut into the patty to see if it is cooked through, but has a melting tenderness. The interior should not be dry. Adjust the oil temperature if necessary. Drop in the remaining batter, several large spoonfuls at a time. Don't crowd the *tortas* as they cook. Repeat the process until all the batter is used.

Transfer the patties to a platter and top with chile sauce, or offer the sauce on the side. Serve immediately.

Fried Potatoes

These simple tubers blanketed in savory red chile make a hearty morning eye-opener.

Makes 6 servings

4 or 5 medium russet potatoes
3 tablespoons oil, preferably corn
  or canola
1 tablespoon minced white onion,
  optional

Salt to taste
½ cup Red Chile Sauce (See recipe,
  page 62)

Although the best-known historical reference to potatoes is probably in connection with the Irish, the tubers are actually a New World crop, cultivated by the Incas thousands of years ago.

Wash the potatoes and prick them with a fork. Bake the potatoes in a medium oven until they are tender. Remove the potatoes and set them aside to cool. Cut the baked potatoes, unpeeled, into bite-size chunks.

Heat the oil in a heavy medium skillet (cast iron is especially good) and add the onion, if desired. Sauté briefly over medium heat until the onion wilts. Add the potatoes to the skillet, sautéing until the chunks begin to turn brown and just a little crusty. Add more oil if the potatoes begin clinging to the pan. Salt to taste.

Transfer the potatoes to a plate or dish and pour warm red chile sauce over them. Serve immediately.

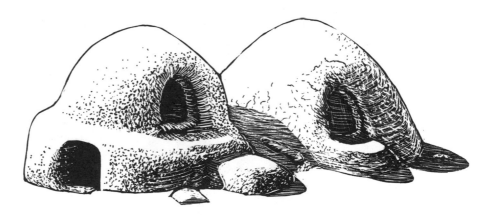

Queso de Cabra
Goat Cheese

If you don't like the more pronounced flavor of goat's milk, or can't locate a suitable source, the queso *can be made with whole or skimmed cow's milk, or with cream. Just make sure that the product is not ultra-pasteurized, a process that cooks the milk so thoroughly that it will not coagulate.*

For optimum safety, buy only goat's milk that comes from a reputable, certified dairy. It is often found in health food stores.

Well into the twentieth century, cheesemaking in New Mexico was as regular a chore as bread baking. The cheese was generally soft and uncured, made from goat's milk. Families saved liquid rennet from the stomachs of butchered goats. When the rennet was added to milk, an enzyme in the rennet caused coagulation and the formation of curds. Now commercial rennet tablets make this process a snap. The Jaramillos' friend Nolia Martinez developed this simple contemporary recipe and still makes the cheese regularly. Mrs. Martinez serves the fresh, mild cheese as a side dish to be eaten with tortillas, or as a dessert with fruit. She sometimes sweetens the cheese with a touch of honey or molasses.

Note: A cheesecloth is needed for this recipe.

Makes approximately 12 ounces of cheese

½ gallon goat's milk (not ultra-pasteurized)

4 junket rennet tablets (available in the baking section of many supermarkets)

1 tablespoon water

In a large saucepan, heat the milk to 110°. If the milk gets too hot, it can be cooled back down to the proper temperature.

While the milk is heating, crush the junket rennet tablets with the back of a spoon and dissolve them in the water.

When the milk reaches the proper temperature, remove the pan from the heat, add the rennet liquid, and quickly stir. Then leave the pan undisturbed for 10 to 20 minutes. While the milk is setting into a thick curd-like custard, line a colander or large strainer with 2 thicknesses of cheesecloth. Set the colander where the milk mixture will be able to drain at room temperature for at least 4 hours or overnight. After the custard has set 10 to 20 minutes, stir it—it will be stiff—and spoon it into the colander. Leave it undisturbed, so that the whey will drain from the curds. The watery whey can be discarded, or added to soups or stocks for extra protein.

The completed cheese can be loosely molded into a round. Store it, refrigerated, in the damp cheesecloth, overwrapped in plastic. The cheese keeps up to a week. Remove the cheese from the refrigerator about 30 minutes before serving.

PAN
Bread

Sopaipillas

Light, airy pillows of fried bread are the pride of Rancho de Chimayó. The golden puffs of dough accompany all meals. They can be stuffed with savory or sweet fillings. Part of the restaurant's secret is frying the *sopaipillas* in hotter oil than can be safely recommended to the home cook. The recipe has been altered slightly for successful home use. Exclude the sugar if the fried breads are to be used for *sopaipillas rellenas*.

The restaurant makes its dough twice a day by hand and cooks the billowy *sopaipillas* to order. On a busy summer day, the staff serves nearly 4,000 *sopaipillas*.

Note: A cooking thermometer that registers up to at least 410° is required for this recipe.

Makes 12 sopaipillas

2 cups flour
1 teaspoon salt
1 teaspoon baking powder
1½ teaspoons sugar, optional
1½ teaspoons oil, preferably canola or corn
½ cup lukewarm water

¼ cup evaporated milk, at room temperature
Oil, preferably canola or corn, for deep-frying, to a depth of 2 inches
Honey, as an accompaniment

If you are cooking at 6,500 to 7,500 feet altitude, decrease the baking powder by ½ teaspoon and reduce the oil temperature by 10°. At altitudes between 2,500 and 6,500 feet, adjust the baking powder and temperature accordingly.

Rice bran oil, long used in Japanese tempura frying, has become available in more areas in the 1990s. The tasteless, odorless oil is especially stable when frying at high temperatures. Try it for so-paipillas if you find it in the supermarket.

Sift together the flour, salt, baking powder, and, if desired, sugar into a large mixing bowl. Into the dry ingredients, pour the oil and mix with fingertips to combine. Add the water and the milk, working the liquids into the dough until a sticky ball forms.

Lightly dust a counter or pastry board with flour, and knead the dough vigorously for 1 minute. The mixture should be "earlobe" soft and no longer sticky. Let the dough rest, covered with a damp cloth, for 15 minutes. Divide the dough into 3 balls, cover the balls with the damp cloth, and let them rest for another 15 to 30 minutes. If not for use immediately, the dough can be refrigerated up to 4 hours.

Dust a counter or pastry board lightly with flour, and roll out each ball of dough into a circle or oval approximately ¼ inch thick. Trim off any ragged edges and discard them. To avoid toughening the dough, it should only be rolled out once. With a sharp knife, cut each circle of the dough into 4 wedges. Cover the wedges with the damp cloth. Don't stack the wedges, because they are likely to stick together.

Layer several thicknesses of paper towels near the stove. In a wok or a high-sided, heavy skillet, heat the oil to 400°. Give the oil your full attention so that, while it is heating, the temperature does not exceed 400°. If the oil smokes before reaching the proper temperature, it cannot be used for this recipe, because there is a danger of it catching fire. Make sure you are using fresh, high-quality oil.

Exercising care to avoid a possible burn, gently drop a wedge of dough into the hot oil. After sinking in the oil briefly, it should begin to balloon and rise back to the surface. Cautiously spoon some of the oil over the *sopaipilla* after it begins to float. When the top surface has fully puffed, a matter of seconds, turn the *sopaipilla* over with tongs, again being extremely cautious. Cook it until it is just light golden, remove it with tongs, and drain it on paper towels. If a *sopaipilla* darkens before it is fully puffed, decrease the temperature by a few degrees before frying the remaining dough. Make 2 to 3 *sopaipillas* at a time, adjusting the heat as necessary to keep the oil's temperature consistent. Drain the fried breads on the paper towels. Arrange them in a napkin-lined basket and serve immediately with honey.

Flour Tortillas

Makes 6 tortillas, approximately 7 inches in diameter

2 cups flour
1 teaspoon salt
1 teaspoon baking powder
1½ teaspoons oil, preferably canola
   or corn

½ cup lukewarm water
¼ cup evaporated milk, at room
   temperature

Sift together the flour, salt, and baking powder into a large mixing bowl. Into the dry ingredients, pour the oil and mix with your fingertips to combine. Add the water and milk, working the liquids into the dough until a sticky ball forms.

Lightly dust a counter or pastry board with flour and knead the dough vigorously for 1 minute. The mixture should be "earlobe" soft and no longer sticky. Let the dough rest, covered with a damp cloth, for about 15 minutes. Divide the dough into 6 balls, cover them again with the damp cloth, and let them rest for another 15 to 30 minutes. If not for use immediately, the dough can be refrigerated up to 4 hours.

Dust a counter or pastry board lightly with flour and roll out each ball of dough into a circle or oval approximately ¼ inch thick. A tortilla roller is easier to use than a conventional rolling pin. Trim off any ragged edges and discard them. To avoid toughening the dough, it should only be rolled out once.

Heat a dry griddle or heavy skillet over high heat for 5 minutes. Cook the tortillas 30 seconds on each side, or until the dough looks dry and slightly wrinkled, and a few brown speckles form on both surfaces. Serve warm in a napkin-lined basket, or reserve for another use.

At higher altitudes, decrease the baking powder by ¼ teaspoon.

As modern cooks, we take baking powder for granted, spooning a little out from the pantry when needed. Baked goods used to be leavened with tequesquite *(sometimes spelled* texquite*), a pumice-like substance containing sodium nitrate. Found in New Mexico's rocky heights, te-quesquite was ground and soaked in water. The resulting liquid, strained, helped breads rise.*

Corn Tortillas

For blue corn tortillas, substitute 1 cup of blue corn flour (maiz de azul) for 1 cup of the masa harina.

Note: A tortilla press is needed to make this recipe, unless you know someone who has years of experience patting out tortillas by hand.

Makes 1 dozen 5- to 6-inch tortillas

2 cups *masa harina*, or more as needed

1 cup plus 2 tablespoons warm water, or more as needed

Salt to taste, optional

Heat a dry griddle or heavy skillet over medium heat.

In a large bowl, mix the ingredients with a sturdy spoon or your hands until the dough is smooth and forms a ball. The dough should be quite moist, but hold its shape. Add a little more water or *masa harina*, if needed, to achieve the proper consistency.

Form the dough into 12 balls approximately 1½ inches in diameter. Cover the balls with plastic wrap to keep them from drying out. If any of the balls do dry out before cooking, knead more water into them. Unlike the dough for flour tortillas, this dough can be reworked.

Place one ball of dough between the two sheets of plastic sometimes sold with the tortilla press, or use two heavyweight plastic sandwich bags. Press the ball in the tortilla press until it is flattened to the desired thickness, usually about ¼ inch. Carefully pull the plastic from the round of dough and lay the dough on the hot griddle or skillet. Cook the tortilla for 30 seconds. Flip it and cook it for 1 minute on its second side. Then flip it back over to cook about 30 seconds longer on the first side. The tortilla will be speckled with brown flecks. Cover the cooked tortillas with foil to keep them warm while the remaining balls of dough are shaped and cooked. Serve immediately in a covered basket.

Chimayó Apple Tequila Jelly

Laura Ann Jaramillo's friend Patsy Swendson created this jelly based on Rancho de Chimayó's famous Chimayó cocktail. It originally appeared in Patsy's cookbook, *Makin' Memories in the Kitchen*, published by Eakin Press.

Note: Jelly jars with new lids and metal bands are needed to prepare this recipe.

Makes 6 ½-pint jars

3½ cups sugar
1¾ cups apple cider, preferably unfiltered
¼ cup Cuervo Gold or other high-quality tequila

2 tablespoons crème de cassis
6 ounces liquid Certo or other liquid fruit pectin

Sterilize the jelly jars and their lids by running them through the dishwasher, or by boiling them in a large pan of water for at least 10 minutes. Keep them in the dishwasher or submerged in the water until they are ready to use.

In the top container of a large double boiler, mix together all the ingredients except the pectin. Place the pan over its water bath and heat the water to a boil. Stir in the pectin and return to a rolling boil for 1 minute. Remove the jelly from the heat. If foam has accumulated on the surface, skim it with a clean spoon. Pour the jelly into the sterilized jars.

Process and seal the jars of jelly using the water-bath method, carefully following the directions that accompany your jars. Store the jelly in a cool place for up to 1 year.

The jelly is a tasty accompaniment to *sopaipillas*, flour tortillas, and other kinds of bread or biscuits. Patsy recommends it with fresh strawberries and Laura likes it over vanilla ice cream.

Generations of home cooks have prepared jelly in any type of clean, lidded jar, sealing the jelly with melted paraffin. As of 1990, safety regulations changed and now these practices are no longer recommended. Only canning jars with new metal lids and screw bands should be used, and processing in a boiling water bath is the only accepted method of sealing and sterilizing the jelly.

Jelly is easy to make, but recipes need to be followed precisely according to their directions and proportions. Never reduce the quantity of sugar. If you desire a larger quantity of jelly, make a separate batch, rather than doubling the recipe.

Pectin, a natural substance found in fruit, causes jelly to gel. Commercial pectin is available in liquid or powdered form, but the two types are not interchangeable.

Flan

One of Rancho de Chimayó's most famous dishes is the caramel-topped, baked custard called flan. The Jaramillo family recipe dates back four generations to a time when canned, evaporated milk was the only type readily available. The canned milk is still used to make this flan distinctively dense. It's a delightful finish to any meal.

Serves 8

FOR THE CUSTARD
2¼ cups canned evaporated milk
   (1½ 12-ounce cans)
1½ cups sugar

¾ cup water
6 eggs
½ teaspoon vanilla

FOR THE CARAMEL
¼ cup sugar

TO PREPARE THE CUSTARD
Preheat the oven to 300°.
   Place all the custard ingredients into a double boiler's top pan. Beat with

After Genoveva Martinez, who helped the Jaramillos open the Restaurante, cook Josie Ortiz has the longest continuous tenure. The affable Josie presides over the stove, as she has almost every morning since 1976, keeping a watchful eye on the sauces and desserts. Making the superb flan in batches of 70 portions is one of her first responsibilities of the day.

a whisk, or with a hand mixer at medium speed, for about 1 minute, or until the mixture is well-blended and begins to froth at its rim.

Insert the pan over its water bath, and heat the mixture over medium-low heat until it is warm throughout. Do not let the custard boil. Keep it warm over a very low flame while preparing the caramel.

TO PREPARE THE CARAMEL

Set 8 custard cups or other heatproof cups on a counter within easy reach of the stove. Have a padded kitchen mitt nearby for use when it is time to pour the caramelized sugar into the cups.

Measure the sugar into a heavy saucepan or skillet no larger than 1 quart. Cook over low heat, watching carefully as the sugar melts into a golden-brown caramel syrup. There is no need to stir unless the sugar is melting unevenly. When the syrup turns a rich medium-brown, don the padded mitt and immediately remove the pan from the heat, using extreme caution. Pour about a teaspoon of caramel into the bottom of each custard cup, continuing to exercise meticulous care. The syrup in the cups will harden almost immediately. The quantity of syrup allows a little extra in case some of it hardens in the pan before you get all 8 cups filled.

To make cleaning easier, place the pan used for liquefying the sugar into a sink and run water in it at once. Stay clear of the steam that will rise as the water hits the hot metal surface.

ASSEMBLING THE FLAN

Pour the warmed custard mixture equally into the cups, and place them in a baking pan large enough to accommodate all of the cups with a little room for air circulation. Add warm water to the pan, enough to cover the bottom third of the cups, and bake 1¾ hours. Check to see if the custard is firm and its top has begun to color a light brown; if not, bake up to 15 minutes more.

Remove the cups from the oven and let them cool 15 to 20 minutes at room temperature. Cover the cups and refrigerate them for at least 3 hours or overnight.

Just prior to serving, take the cups from the refrigerator and uncover them. Unmold the first dessert by running a knife between the custard and the cup. Cover the cup with an individual serving plate and invert, giving the cup a brief shake to loosen. The custard should drop to the plate. If not, try the process again. Repeat for the remaining custards and serve.

Unlike some softer, creamier versions of this dessert, the Rancho de Chimayó flan is a good "make ahead" dish because it improves in flavor and texture for a day. It is good on day 2 as well, but the flavor begins to fade. Custards should not be kept beyond 2 days.

Pumpkin Flan

The authors created this dish, based on the restaurant's traditional flan, to take advantage of Rancho de Chimayó's bounty of fall pumpkins. Canned pumpkin is a fine substitute. This dish requires only the tiniest dab of caramel syrup in each custard cup. When unmolded, the caramel glistens across the top, instead of running down the sides and pooling around the flan. It should complement, not overwhelm, the pumpkin and spices.

Makes 8 to 10 servings

FOR THE CUSTARD

1 2-pound pumpkin, or 1½ cups canned pumpkin purée
1 17-ounce can evaporated milk
5 eggs
1½ cups sugar

4 tablespoons dark rum, preferably Myers's
¾ teaspoon cinnamon
¾ teaspoon dried, ground ginger
⅛ teaspoon nutmeg

FOR THE CARAMEL

2 tablespoons sugar

FOR THE GARNISH

2 tablespoons piñon nuts, lightly toasted

TO PREPARE THE CUSTARD

If you are using fresh pumpkin, preheat the oven to 350°. Rinse the pumpkin and cut it in half crosswise. Remove strings and seeds. Place the pumpkin halves on a baking sheet, cut sides down, and bake them 45 minutes or more, until they are very tender. Remove them from the oven and allow them to cool. When cool enough to handle, scrape the pulp from the skin and force the pulp through a ricer or strainer. Measure 1½ cups of the purée, saving the rest for another use.

Reduce the oven temperature to 300°.

Place all of the custard ingredients into a double boiler's top pan. Whisk, or beat with a hand mixer at medium speed, for about 1 minute, or until the mixture is well-blended and begins to froth at its rim.

Insert the pan over its water bath and heat the mixture over medium-low heat until it is warm throughout. Do not let the custard boil. Keep the custard warm over very low heat while preparing the caramel.

TO PREPARE THE CARAMEL

Set 8 to 10 custard cups on a counter within easy reach of the stove. Have

Shortly after Chimayó colonists harvested their crops in the fall, they headed to the hills to pick piñon nuts. The early settlers discovered the Pueblos harvesting the nuts from a squatty pine that grows in the southern Rockies at altitudes of 4,000 to 7,500 feet. While today's Chimayó residents can buy New Mexican, Italian, or even Chinese pine nuts at the grocery store, many families still prefer to gather their own. The yields are substantial only every fourth or fifth year.

Fallen piñon nuts are first plucked from the ground, then sheets are laid under the trees, which are shaken to loosen more of the tiny nuts. The most stubborn nuts have to be picked out of the pine cones by hand. The nuts are usually stored in their shells in a cool cellar or frozen for later use.

a padded kitchen mitt nearby for use when it is time to pour the caramelized sugar into the cups.

Measure the sugar into a heavy saucepan or skillet, no larger than 1 quart. Cook over low heat, watching carefully as the sugar melts into a golden-brown caramel syrup. There is no need to stir unless the sugar is melting unevenly. When the syrup turns a rich medium-brown, don the padded mitt and immediately remove the pan from the heat, using extreme caution. Pour about ½ teaspoon of caramel into the bottom of each custard cup, continuing to exercise meticulous care. The syrup in the bottom of each cup will harden almost immediately. The quantity of syrup allows a little extra in case some of it hardens in the pan before you can fill all of the cups.

To make cleaning easier, place the pan used for liquefying the sugar into a sink and run water in it at once. Stay clear of the steam that will rise as the water hits the hot metal surface.

ASSEMBLING THE FLAN

Pour the warmed custard mixture equally into the cups, and place them in a baking pan large enough to accommodate all of the cups with a little room for air circulation. Add warm water to the pan, enough to cover the bottom third of the cups. Bake 1 hour and 50 minutes, or until the custard is lightly firm and slightly raised.

Remove the cups from the oven and let them cool 15 to 20 minutes at room temperature. Cover the cups and refrigerate them for at least 3 hours or overnight.

Just prior to serving, take the cups from the refrigerator and uncover them. Unmold the first dessert by running a knife between the custard and the cup. Cover the cup with an individual serving plate and invert, giving the cup a brief shake to loosen. The custard should drop to the plate. If not, try the process again. Repeat for the remaining custards and serve. Top each portion of flan with a sprinkling of the piñon nuts and serve.

Like the original Rancho de Chimayó flan, the pumpkin flan is a good "make ahead" dish because it improves in flavor and texture for a day. It is good on day 2 as well, but its flavor begins to fade. Custards should not be kept beyond 2 days.

Natillas

Thickening puddings and custards with cornstarch was originally a way of extending the precious supply of eggs.

Natillas historically were a "floating island" dessert, with puffs of uncooked meringue dotting the creamy pudding. With current health concerns about raw eggs, Rancho de Chimayó has switched to topping the pudding with whipped cream. Some other contemporary recipes call for poached meringues, but the cooking process can alter the texture and taste of the egg whites. Whipped cream melts on the tongue in a similar fashion to the original topping. The recipe is simple, but allow at least 30 minutes for cooking the pudding. Trying to speed the process can result in a grainy rather than silky texture.

Makes 8 servings

FOR THE PUDDING

8 eggs	1 cup sugar
4 cups (1 quart) milk	½ teaspoon vanilla
3 tablespoons cornstarch	

FOR THE TOPPING

Sweetened whipped cream	Cinnamon

Separate the eggs, placing the yolks into the top pan of a double boiler and saving the whites for another use.

Measure 3 tablespoons of the milk and mix it with the cornstarch. Set aside.

Pour the rest of the milk, the sugar, and the vanilla into the egg yolks. Insert the pan over its water bath. Warm the mixture over medium-low heat, simultaneously whisking, or beating with a hand mixer, just until well-blended. Continue heating the mixture, frequently stirring up from the bottom, until the pudding is somewhat thickened. It will still be runny, but will cling thinly to the back of the spoon. Expect this process to take 20 minutes, maybe longer. Make sure the mixture does not boil. The egg yolks in the pudding should thicken and poach, but not scramble.

Add the reserved cornstarch to the pudding and continue heating. The mixture should quickly begin to thicken, adhering more readily to the spoon. Cook about 5 more minutes, to eliminate any taste of raw cornstarch. Lower the heat, if necessary, to keep the pudding from boiling.

Place a large strainer over a bowl and pour the pudding through the strainer to catch any bits of coagulated egg. Continue to stir the strained pudding for a few minutes to release steam. Cover the pudding and refrigerate it for at least 1 hour, preferably 2 hours.

Just before serving, spoon out individual portions of the pudding and top each with a dollop of whipped cream and a generous sprinkle of cinnamon. Serve chilled.

Natillas can be made a day ahead. Leftovers should be discarded after a couple of days.

Sopaipillas with Cinnamon and Sugar

Makes 6 servings

1 recipe *sopaipillas* (See recipe, page 105)

½ cup sugar
1½ teaspoons cinnamon

Make the *sopaipillas* according to the directions, except cut each dough round into 16 sections rather than 4.

Add the sugar and cinnamon to a medium-sized paper bag. Just after frying each batch of the *sopaipillas*, place them in the bag. Shake the bag to coat the *sopaipillas* with the cinnamon sugar. Repeat with all of the remaining *sopaipillas*. Serve *sopaipillas* immediately on dessert plates, or eat them as finger food.

To streamline the final preparation of the dessert, the dough can be rolled out and cut into sections just before the meal begins. Avoid stacking the sections or they may stick to each other. Cover the dough with a damp cloth, and complete the preparations just before serving.

Biscochitos

New Mexicans take their *biscochitos*, or *bizcochitos*, seriously. They love the delicate anise-scented sugar cookie so much that the legislature was moved to declare it the state cookie. Reminiscent of tender shortbread or a flaky pie crust, the *biscochito* is traditionally associated with the Christmas season. A spice like anise, imported from Spain, used to be costly and was consequently saved for important celebrations.

Lard was the original shortening of choice. While Rancho de Chimayó and most home cooks today don't use lard, it does yield a flakier cookie. Beverly and Fabiola Vigil contributed to this recipe.

Makes about 5 dozen medium-sized cookies

FOR THE TOPPING

⅓ cup sugar   1 teaspoon cinnamon

FOR THE COOKIES

1 cup vegetable shortening or lard   1¾ teaspoons baking powder
½ cup sugar   ½ teaspoon salt
1 egg   2 tablespoons dessert wine,
1½ teaspoons anise seeds   bourbon, or brandy
3 cups flour   Water, as needed

TO PREPARE THE TOPPING

Combine the sugar and cinnamon in a small bowl and set aside.

TO PREPARE THE COOKIES

Preheat the oven to 375°.

In a large mixing bowl, cream the shortening or lard with the sugar until fluffy. Add the egg and the anise seeds and blend them in well. Set aside.

Sift together the flour, baking powder, and salt and add to the shortening and sugar mixture. Mix in the dry ingredients with a pastry cutter or two forks. When a crumbly dough is formed, add the wine or liquor. If the mixture doesn't hold together, add water by the teaspoon until a ball of dough is formed. Add no more water than is necessary; the mixture should just barely bind together. A stiff, pie-crust type of dough is the desired result. Divide the dough into several balls.

Flour a counter or pastry board and roll out the first ball of dough to a ¼-inch thickness. Cut the dough into decorative shapes with a cookie cutter. Repeat with the remaining dough. For the flakiest *biscochitos*, try not to reroll and handle the dough any more than is absolutely necessary. Place all of the cookies on ungreased baking sheets and sprinkle them with up to half of the reserved cinnamon sugar.

Bake the cookies in the preheated oven for about 10 to 12 minutes, or until light golden-brown. Remove the cookies from the oven and sprinkle them again with the remaining cinnamon sugar. Set aside on absorbent paper to cool.

Serve *biscochitos* immediately or cover tightly for later use. *Biscochitos* keep satisfactorily for a week. They also freeze well for up to several months.

Sopaipilla Cream Puffs

Advance planning can make sopaipilla cream puffs less complex for the home cook to orchestrate. Before the meal begins, roll out and cut the sopaipilla dough and cover the pieces with a damp cloth. Don't stack the pieces or they may stick together. Pour the oil needed for frying into a pan. Whip the cream until stiff and refrigerate it along with the natillas pudding. As dishes for the main course are cleared, heat the oil for frying and ready the dessert plates. The final preparation time can then be a reasonable interval for the host's or hostess's absence from the dinner table.

A modern pairing of two northern New Mexico classics, the elegant *sopaipilla* cream puffs were inspired by a Texas dentist who saved the fried bread served with his main dish to combine with his favorite dessert. The warm, flaky *sopaipillas* contrast dramatically with the cool, silky *natillas*. The combination makes a memorable conclusion to any meal.

Makes 6 servings

½ recipe *Sopaipillas* (See recipe, page 105)
½ recipe *Natillas* pudding (See recipe, page 115)

Whipped cream
Cinnamon, optional, for garnish

With a serrated knife, carefully slice each *sopaipilla* in half, creating two pockets of the fried bread. Spoon about ¼ cup of the *natillas* pudding into each pocket. Repeat with the remaining *sopaipilla* halves.

Arrange the pudding-filled *sopaipillas* on dessert plates, and top each with a generous dollop of whipped cream. Dust with cinnamon, if desired. Serve immediately.

Panocha

Generations of Jaramillos and other native New Mexicans have served panocha, a thick, rich dessert similar to Indian pudding, during the Lenten season and for Easter dinner. Long cooking results in a heavy pudding colored a lustrous dark brown. It requires a special sprouted wheat flour that is not widely available, but can be acquired from several mail-order sources (see the last chapter). Supplies of panocha flour are best in the late winter and early spring, around the time of Lent. Cook Loida Ortiz makes an especially tasty version of panocha for the Restaurante.

Note: Making the panocha in a smaller quantity doesn't work very well. It keeps, refrigerated, for a week, or can be easily frozen.

Makes 15 to 20 servings

2½ cups *harina enraizada* (panocha flour)	4½ cups water
1¼ cups flour	½ cup dark brown sugar
	Cream, optional, for topping

Sift each flour separately, and then sift the two together into a large, heavy saucepan. Up to a few teaspoons of the panocha flour will likely be too coarse for sifting. Discard any coarse flour that remains in the sifter.

In a second pan, bring the water to a boil. Add the brown sugar to the water and stir to dissolve. Pour the water cup by cup into the flour, stirring well after each addition. When all the water is incorporated and no lumps remain, the mixture should resemble Cream of Wheat cereal. Cover the panocha and let it sit for 15 to 20 minutes.

While the mixture sits, preheat the oven to 300°. Butter a large covered baking dish and set it aside.

Uncover the panocha and bring it to a boil over medium heat. Reduce the heat to a simmer, and cook for 30 minutes, stirring frequently. The texture of the pudding will change during the cooking time from grainy to somewhat silky, and the color will deepen. It will be sticky.

Pour the panocha into the prepared baking dish and place the dish in the oven. Bake, covered, stirring after the first hour. The total baking time will be 2 to 2½ hours, or until the pudding cooks down by about one quarter. Serve the panocha warm, in very small portions, topped with cream if desired.

If you are cooking at a high altitude, start the recipe with an additional ½ cup of water. A longer cooking time, 3 to 3½ hours, will probably be required. Stir each hour while baking, checking the thickness of the pudding.

Panocha was probably the first dessert prepared by the original Chimayó settlers. Sugar wasn't yet readily available and honey was too scarce for them to use in quantity. By wetting whole wheat, though, and setting it in a warm spot to sprout, some of the wheat's starch was converted to sugar, giving flour ground from the grain a natural sweetness. A dish made just from the flour could satisfy a sweet tooth. Some cooks still prepare panocha without adding sugar.

Contemporary additions to panocha include a teaspoon or so of cinnamon and/or vanilla. A tablespoon or two of butter gives extra richness, too. Any of these additions should be made at the conclusion of the panocha's cooking time on the stove, just prior to baking. Whipped cream can top the dessert as well.

Capirotada

Many cultures have some variation of bread pudding. The traditional recipes in northern New Mexico usually differ from those elsewhere in the lack of eggs and the addition of cheese. Because *capirotada* originated as a special holiday dessert, sugar was used liberally to make a very sweet dish. This is the Jaramillos' favorite version.

Makes 6 servings

FOR THE SYRUP

2½ cups water

1 cup brown sugar

2 cloves

1 stick cinnamon

FOR THE PUDDING

Butter

8 slices white bread

1 cup grated mild cheddar cheese

½ cup raisins

½ cup piñon nuts

TO PREPARE THE SYRUP

Combine all of the ingredients in a small saucepan and simmer over medium heat for about 15 minutes, until the mixture has cooked down by about one quarter. Remove the cloves and cinnamon. Set the syrup aside to cool.

TO PREPARE THE PUDDING

Preheat the oven to 350°. Butter a shallow medium-sized baking dish and set it aside.

Tear the bread into bite-size pieces, and spread the pieces on a baking sheet. Toast the bread in the oven for 10 to 15 minutes, turning occasionally, until dry and slightly browned.

Layer ½ of the the toast pieces, cheese, raisins, and piñon nuts, then repeat for a second layer. Slowly ladle the reserved syrup over the layers, making sure that the toast pieces are soaked well. Gently press the toast into the syrup. Bake for 30 to 40 minutes, or until the syrup is absorbed and the *capirotada* has a creamy, almost custard-like consistency.

Serve warm. *Capirotada* can be assembled up to 6 hours in advance and refrigerated. Bring the dish back to room temperature before proceeding with baking. Leftovers can be refrigerated for a couple of days and gently reheated.

Chimayó residents often add some of their noted apples to capirotada. *Pare one of your favorite apples, slice it into small chunks, and sauté it lightly in a tablespoon of butter. Add the sautéed apple to the layers of bread and other ingredients.*

Suggested Special Menus

EASTER CELEBRATION

A joyous conclusion to the solemnity of Lent, Easter signifies rebirth and renewal. The typical Easter meal in northern New Mexico includes an egg dish to symbolize new life and other fresh dishes like greens and goat cheese. The feast usually features *cabrito*, young goat, roasted in a pit, on a spit, or in the oven as the recipe in the book recommends.

Green Salad with House Dressing
Cabrito
Torta de Huevo Tradicional with Red Chile Sauce
Calabacitas
Queso de Cabra
Chimayó Apple Tequila Jelly
Flour Tortillas
Panocha or Natillas

CHIMAYÓ BRUNCH

Gonzalo Specials
Huevos Rancheros or Torta de Huevo con Chile y Carne
"Refried" Beans
Café Español

THE JAMISONS' COMBINATION

A selection of some of the authors' favorite dishes.

Grand Gold Margaritas
Burrell Tortilla
Burrito Al Estilo Madril with Vegetable Garnish
Pinto Beans
Posole
Flan

SUMMER WEDDING

Few places are more attractive for an afternoon wedding reception than the patio terraces at Rancho de Chimayó. A substantial and festive menu is generally a part of the nuptial celebration. For more information on traditional engagements and weddings, see page 16.

Chile con Queso and Tostadas
Chicken Flautas with Guacamole and Salsa
Fruit Salad Plate
Fresh Vegetable Plate (4 to 6 kinds of the freshest raw vegetables available,
arranged decoratively on a platter)
Flour Tortillas
Sopaipilla Cream Puffs
Margaritas
Chimayó Cocktail Punch

ANNIVERSARY DINNER

Chimayó Cocktails
Carne Asada
Rolled Cheese Enchilada with Green Chile Sauce
"Refried" Beans
Flan
Café Mexicano

VEGETARIAN OPTIONS

Laura Ann Jaramillo abstains from eating all meat and animal products. She makes sure that the restaurant menu includes a variety of options for other vegetarians and for anyone who likes an occasional meatless meal. These are two of Laura's suggested meals.

Tomato Salsa
Tostadas
Bean Burritos with Vegetarian Red Chile Sauce
Calabacitas
Sopaipillas with Cinnamon and Sugar

Green Salad with House Dressing
Zucchini–Green Chile Tamales with Vegetarian Green Chile Sauce
Spanish Rice
Capirotada

HARVEST DINNER

This meal showcases the flavors of fall in the Chimayó Valley.

Chimayó Cocktails or Chilled Apple Cider
Pico de Gallo and Tostadas
Carne Adovada
Posole
Roasted Green Chile
Sopaipillas
Pumpkin Flan

LAS POSADAS SUPPER

The *Las Posadas* pageant is acted out on each of the nine nights before Christmas. Parishioners portray Mary and Joseph going from door to door, commemorating the Holy Family's futile search for lodging at Bethlehem inns prior to the birth of Christ. One home finally welcomes and shelters the couple, laying out a hearty and festive mid-evening supper for all the participating villagers. The traditional Chimayó dishes are listed here. For more information about *Las Posadas*, see page 17.

Cidre Caliente
Pinto Beans
Posole
Red and Green Chile Sauces
Flour Tortillas
Biscochitos

CHRISTMAS DINNER

The celebratory Christmas feast is usually served at about 2 A.M., following Midnight Mass. For more information about Christmas customs, see pages 17–19.

Cidre Caliente con Tuaca
Ensalada de Noche Buena
Pork Tamales
Posole
Red and Green Chile Sauces
Sopaipillas
Chimayó Apple Tequila Jelly
Natillas or Biscochitos

New Mexico Products & Mail-Order Sources

Despite the fact that Rancho de Chimayó's cooking and northern New Mexican cooking are different from what is found in almost any other area of the United States, the great majority of ingredients and products are familiar to most home cooks. The items briefly explained below are associated specifically with New Mexican, Southwestern, and Mexican food, and could be unusual to anyone who may not already be acquainted with those styles of cooking.

CHILE

When New Mexicans refer to chile they are talking about pungent pods, or sauce made from those pods, not the concoction of spices, meat, and/or beans known as Texas chili con carne. While chile, the pod, is sometimes spelled chili, chilli, or chillie elsewhere, U.S. Senator Pete Domenici of New Mexico made this state's spelling official by entering it into the *Congressional Record*.

The New Mexico State Legislature jumped into the act, too, declaring chile the state vegetable. They got the spelling right, but in their enthusiasm they missed the fact that chile is a fruit. It's actually more closely related to the tomato than to black pepper, after which it was misnamed. Properly called *capsicums*, chiles range in type from mild bell peppers to the incendiary Habaneros.

To tone down the heat of any chile, remove the seeds and, more importantly, the light-colored veins running the length of the pod. Use this process, or a milder variety of chile, rather than reducing the amount of chile, if you desire a tamer result.

Always keep chile away from your eyes, and never touch your eyes or contact lenses after handling any type of the pods. Rubber gloves are recommended, particularly if your skin is sensitive. Should you need to relieve a burning sensation, Jean Andrews, the author of *Peppers*, suggests a brief wash of your hands in a solution of 5 parts water and 1 part chlorine bleach. Then wash your hands well with soap and water.

Despite their reputation for being hard on the gastrointestinal system, medical research disputes the legend. Actually chiles are healthful, and low in calories too. Green pods come loaded with vitamin C and red pods, even dried, have a high vitamin A content.

The New Mexico chile is a type of capsicum that originated in the state and forms the basis for much of New Mexican cookery. Different varieties of New Mexican pods have different levels of heat, but all are flavorful. New Mexico chiles are harvested while green, or immature, or a few weeks later when the pods have turned crimson. Both types of New Mexico chiles are described below.

NEW MEXICO GREEN CHILE

New Mexico green is used fresh or frozen, and it is usually chopped. In this book, it is added unadorned to guacamole and *chile con queso*, and it is made into a sauce that blankets many of Rancho de Chimayó's other dishes. Around New Mexico, green chile is regularly added to everything from tuna salad to pizza.

Supermarkets nationally have increasing assortments of fresh chiles and may carry New Mexico-type pods, perhaps under the name Anaheim (a widely-used misnomer). They can also be ordered fresh from several of the mail-order sources during the New Mexico harvest season, approximately August to October.

If you purchase fresh chiles, they must first be roasted to blister the tough skins. There are many ways to accomplish this at home, but we recommend two. One method is over a gas burner, the same way marshmallows are roasted over a fire. Spear the chiles on a long-handled fork, place them near the flame, and heat them until the skins have blistered and darkened uniformly. The second method is better for roasting more than one or two chiles at a time. Place a layer of pods on a baking sheet and broil until all are dark, turning the chiles frequently.

Following roasting by either method, place the hot chiles in a plastic or paper bag to steam. Let the chiles cool in the closed bag. Peel the roasted pods if you want to use them immediately. If you plan to freeze the chile, there is no need to remove the skins. The pods will peel easily after freezing.

If this sounds like too much work, or your timing is just wrong, several of the mail-order sources ship frozen green chile already roasted, peeled, and chopped. Any grocery store in New Mexico generally has a stock of frozen green chile in tubs ranging in size from 8 ounces to 5 pounds. Packaged mild or hot, you choose your level of spice. The Restaurante uses half mild and half hot to obtain a good balance of flavor and heat.

Canned green chile is not recommended. The canning process robs the chile of its texture and adds an acidic preservative. Also, canned chile is usually among the blandest of varieties. In an emergency, it can be substituted in *chile con queso* and guacamole, but it would make a totally unworthy version of green chile sauce.

There is now a dried version of green chile receiving increasingly wider distribution. Roasted and peeled before dehydration, it is expensive but good.

The source of New Mexico's finest green chile, and of Rancho de Chimayó's green, is the Mesilla Valley in the southern part of the state.

NEW MEXICO RED CHILE

New Mexico red is most frequently used in the dried form. Traditionally, fresh pods are strung up to dry in colorful *ristras* like those that line the front of Rancho de Chimayó. After the sun and low humidity work their magic, the pods can be used whole or ground. Rancho de Chimayó puts whole pods in the sauce for the *carne adovada*, and ground chile in its other red sauces. Ground red chile should not be confused with chili powder, a totally different product.

Wine aficionados know that the weather and soil in the Bordeaux region of France combine to make a superlative grape. Among connoisseurs, New Mexico red chile grown in Chimayó has a similar stature, renowned for its delicious balance of sweetness and heat. The restaurant acquires its pods just down the road.

Dried red chiles can be found with increasing frequency throughout the United States. Substitute ground New Mexico chile for whole pods if necessary. Dried *ancho* chiles can take the place of New Mexico chiles, although the flavor will be a little different. New Mexico red, in a range of heat, can be ordered easily by mail, and will keep indefinitely if stored in the freezer.

JALAPEÑOS

Especially popular in Tex-Mex cooking and ballpark nachos, jalapeños are this country's best known chile, widely available both fresh and pickled. Fresh *serrano* chiles can substitute, but they are somewhat hotter. Adjust the amount you use accordingly. If you use pickled jalapeños, rinse the vinegar solution from them first.

CHILE PEQUIN

The small, fiery *chile pequin* is used dried and judiciously. If you have trouble locating it, *chile de arbol*, or the more widely available cayenne, can substitute.

CILANTRO

The fresh aromatic leaves of the coriander plant, cilantro is also called Chinese parsley. It doesn't dry well, nor can it be replaced by coriander seed. Sold in produce sections in bunches, cilantro is highly perishable. There are various methods recommended for its storage. We think it keeps best if stored in the refrigerator with its stems in a cup of water and its leaves loosely covered with a plastic bag.

BLUE CORN

This Indian corn, dark blue in color, makes a blue-gray meal when ground. Blue corn has a higher protein content than yellow or white corn, but less starch, making tortillas made from it more fragile. The flavor of blue corn tortillas is a little nuttier than regular tortillas.

PINTO BEANS

A staple of the Southwestern diet since pre-colonial days, the inexpensive pinto is a variety of the kidney bean. Splotches of pinkish-brown give the bean its name, but its spotty color is lost when cooked. Some of the best pinto beans come from New Mexico's Estancia Valley and Colorado's San Luis Valley. The Restaurante recipes call for dried beans, although they are also sold canned.

JÍCAMA

Jícama is a bulbous root vegetable available throughout much of the Southwest, in some large supermarkets nationally, and in Hispanic or Latino markets. Its brown peel shields a white interior with the texture of a water chestnut or apple. The mild flavor is vaguely sweet. It is used at Rancho de Chimayó uncooked.

MASA HARINA

The cornmeal used for tamale and corn tortilla dough is known as *masa harina* (literally "dough flour"). The special meal is ground from dried corn that has been treated with lime. Quaker markets the most widely available brand, found anywhere with a Hispanic or Latino population.

PANOCHA FLOUR

A special sprouted-wheat flour, panocha is used in the Lenten and Easter dessert of the same name. Also known as *harina enraizada*, the flour is sweeter and rougher in texture than regular wheat flours. It can be found in northern New Mexican grocery stores throughout Lent, but it is not always easy to find outside of the season. Readers in other areas will likely need to order it from one of the mail-order sources.

PIÑON NUTS

The indigenous piñon pine dots northern New Mexico's foothills and yields these flavorful nuts. Found in the pine cones, some of the tiny nuts fall to the ground and others must be forced from the cones. Either way the process for collecting them is laborious, and shelling them is almost as difficult, justifying the high prices charged for the nuts.

Piñon nuts found in supermarkets often come from Italy or China and are usually called pignolia or pine nuts. High in fat and extremely rich in flavor, the nuts turn rancid quickly at room temperature. Frozen shelled nuts, though, keep 6 to 9 months.

POSOLE

Dried corn kernels treated with lime are known as *posole*. The term also refers to the dish created with the corn, served at the restaurant generally as a starchy accompaniment, but also frequently used as a festive main dish when dressed up with pork and additional seasonings. *Posole* is sold dried, or pre-soaked and frozen, and is widely available in the Southwest. Canned hominy is an acceptable substitute, but mail-ordering dried *posole* is worth the effort if you are a fan of the dish.

MAIL-ORDER SOURCES

The selected sources listed here are reputable New Mexico businesses, all owner-managed or family-owned and operated. While we can't guarantee they'll stay in business forever, their records of service and delivery are quite good.

Santa Fe School of Cooking
116 West San Francisco Street
Santa Fe, NM 87501
505-983-4511

Catalog available, $10 minimum charge-card order.
Dried chiles, fresh New Mexico green chile in season, full range of other New Mexico products and seasonings, tortilla presses and rollers, serving pieces, cookbooks, gift baskets, traditional New Mexican cooking classes, retail store.

The Chile Shop
109 East Water Street
Santa Fe, NM 87501
505-983-6080

Catalog available, $10 minimum mail order.
Dried chiles, fresh New Mexico green chile in season, good range of other New Mexico products and seasonings, serving pieces, cookbooks, gift baskets, retail store.

My Santa Fe Connection
Post Office Box 1863
Corrales, NM 87048
505-842-9564

Catalog available.
Dried chiles, fresh New Mexico green chile in season, good range of other New Mexico products and seasonings, tortilla presses, cookbooks, gift baskets.

Old Southwest Trading Company
Post Office Box 7545
Albuquerque, NM 87194
800-748-2861
Fax: 505-836-1682

Catalog available, $15 minimum charge-card order.
Dried chiles, fresh New Mexico green chile in season, good range of other New Mexico products and seasonings, tortilla presses, cookbooks, gift baskets.

Los Chileros de Nuevo Mexico
Post Office Box 6215
Santa Fe, NM 87502
505-471-6967

Brochure available.

Dried chiles, fresh New Mexico green chile in season, frozen New Mexico green chile year-round, good range of other New Mexico products and seasonings, gift baskets.

Léona's de Chimayó
Post Office Box 579
Chimayó, NM 87522
505-351-4660

Price list available. Pork and vegetarian tamales, flour tortillas (regular, whole wheat, and many flavors).

Hatch Chile Express
Post Office Box 350
Hatch, NM 87937
505-267-3226

Price list available. Dried chiles, fresh New Mexico green chile in season, frozen New Mexico green chile year-round, retail store.

INDEX